WORDSMITH

A story on creativity, writing skills, problem solving, and strategic risks

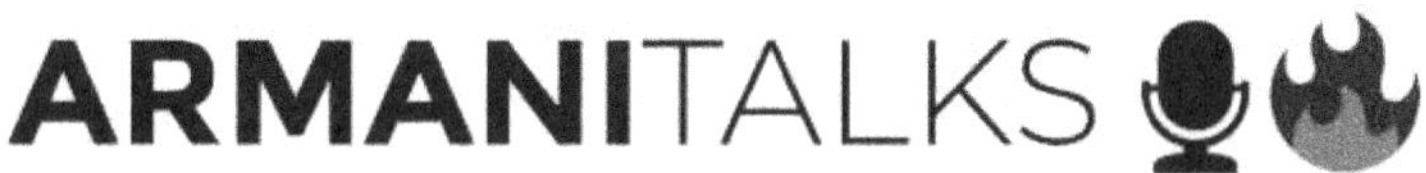

1

Embarrassment wasn't quite the right word for it.

Mortifying would have been better.

Something like this didn't happen to Cason's family. Where they are from, it was honesty, work ethic, and a strong brand presence. But now, Cason's blunder was enough to tear the family name down for lineages.

Eventually, the family would recover. The question is, would Cason recover?

Television watch rates were at an all-time high. Culture is intact like no other era. They say that when the consumers are watching television, then there is an invisible glue to society. It's because people love talking. More importantly, they love talking about what they just watched.

When a show became popular out of nowhere, that's when that show would be spilling over to the water coolers, classrooms, and the workspace.

After the recent surge of television shows based on reality, the network producers had the bright idea for another show.

DUI Dummies.

The name is catchy enough. The concept is even catchier. Record a drunk driver's interaction with the cops.

The pilot episode confirmed the network producers' initial thoughts.

The show was a hit.

Seeing drunk drivers getting pulled over as they were bumbling and stumbling to explain themselves became comedy gold. What was even funnier was how they would interact with the cops. The police officers were stern and meant business. When they were talking to these drunk drivers, there was clearly a power imbalance which made it hilarious.

The show even had an element of unifying the viewers with a common enemy. DUI Dummies got inspiration from the show, How to Catch a Predator. Where there were sting operations to catch predators who were trying to meet up with a 15-year-old girl.

The viewers in unison often felt:
'Well, I'm happy to see that creep off the streets!'

The common sentiment built brand loyalty for the show. That's when the networker producer realized they could do the same with DUI Dummies. I mean, who wouldn't hate someone who got behind the wheel after drinking?

'Well, I'm happy to see these malicious drunks off the streets!'
That was the common sentiment.
All types of people were caught on DUI Dummies.

- Doctors.
- Students.
- Lawyers.

The show caught tons of people in the recording, however, only a few people would be chosen for the final cut.

Cason was one of them.

The sad thing is that Cason is not a partying kind of guy. He's heavily introverted, shy, and a pushover. Picture a people pleaser, and Cason is the person that often comes to people's minds.

He had a bright future growing up.
The kind of kid who was gifted in his academic studies but was average in everything else.

Average when it came to talking to girls.
Average in sports.
And average in looks.

His academic success was supposed to allow him to become a top-level accountant. From there, he was supposed to get married, have kids, by a house etc. The typical American dream.

The day that Cason was caught on DUI Dummies, it felt like his world stopped. Leading up to the release of the show, he got the contact information of the producers. He begged, no seriously, BEGGED the producers to not put him on the show.

He notified them how he was rarely a partyer, and this was not something that he was used to doing. He also notified the producers that he was the son of one of Virginia's finest criminal lawyers.
Cason was the son of *Enzo Enclosed.*

Enclosed was a nickname to show how many cases he closed with ease. Cason was also the son of Michelle Makeup. A popular brand mogul that sold women's fashion products.

Cason was also the little brother of Billy. No cool nickname for Billy, but that didn't take away form Billy's flash as well. Billy was an entrepreneur who owned a herd of ecommerce shops that made him a 6-figure earner at the ripe age of 26.

The producers ensured that Cason had nothing to worry about.

'Kid, listen to us. We have tons of people that we can use on the show. No offense, but your reaction wasn't even spicy! It was a tad bit...boring. You got nothing to worry about.'

When the producer told Cason that, that's when his heartbeat started firing through the roof. Because Cason knew his reaction was THAT BAD.

When he was caught for drunk driving by the police officers, he started off lying. When the officers raised their voice to tell him to stop lying, Cason began crying.

Sobbing about:
*'Trust me officer, **I never** do this. My entire life will be ruined if you don't let me off with a warning.'*

That whimpering turned into horror when one of the officers introduced a host who said:
'Cason, I have to tell you... You are a part of our new TV show, DUI Dummies.'

That's when a herd of cameras surrounded the drunk Cason and he broke down in tears.

The idea of that vulnerable position being shown on national television terrified him. Especially with the show being aired on a mainstream channel.

All he did leading up to the episode release was pray and hope that nothing happened to him. It made the situation worse that his household was in a great mood.

Enzo, Michelle, and Billy had a string of wins in their life and all they could do was highlight how Cason looked sick and worried.

'Everything okay, son? You've been quiet lately. Your face has been looking shriveled too,' said Michelle.

'Yes mom, I'm okay. Just got a few things on my mind.'

He can still recall the day the show was released.

He was hanging out with his parents and brother in the living room and enjoying the television shows. That's when DUI Dummies was about to come on. Cason aggressively began telling his dad to watch Everybody Loves Raymond.

'Come on dad, let's watch Everybody Loves Raymond. Remember how much we used to watch that growing up?'

Cason's dad was not having it. He said:
'We watch that show all the time! I have all the lines memorized by now. I want to watch these scumbags get caught on that DUI show!'

The other 2 in the household agreed, outnumbering Cason 3-1. But Cason wasn't ready to give up.

'Hey, I see Snow White is on. Mom, didn't you love that movie as a kid?'

Hitting his mom's nostalgia was a lethal move that could possibly alter what was about to happen.

'You know what, I did! That was one of the shows I recall watching with your grandma.'

An emotional look came over his mom's face. Especially because his grandma had been sick. He could just poke a little further to make it happen.
'Yea mom. How about Snow White? It's about to start....'

She thought about it.

Then she quickly pulled the trigger. She looked at her husband and said:
'Hey, we can watch the rerun of DUI Dummies another time. Please, can we watch Snow White??'

Enzo fought for a little. But it was not enough to overpower his wife's puppy dog eyes. She won and they changed the channel to Snow White.

Just another day that Cason could relax.

'I'm definitely overthinking. I've been able to do such a good job in hiding the DUI so far. What makes me think from all the other people in the US, that I'm going to be one of the rare few who gets caught on the show?'

40 minutes passes by.

That's when Cason's parents and his brother's phones begin lighting up. That's when Cason's phone begins lighting up too...

His heart sank.
A bunch of texts on his phone.
'Hey bro! I just saw you on TV. You good?'
'What the fuck dude, did you really drive drunk??'
'I can't believe you, Cason. You're normally so responsible.'

As he was getting bombed with texts and calls from his coworkers, cousins, and friends...his parents and brother looked at him.

'Cason, what did you do?' asked Billy in a mortified voice.

All Cason could do was hang his head in shame.

The months after that had been brutal.

He got fired from his job, the townspeople would blatantly gossip about him, and his parents couldn't even look him in the eyes.

Their son had bought dishonor to the family and they could do nothing about it. The days after the showing of DUI Dummies was intense.

Billy would come into Cason's room every now and then to say that:
'Everything would be okay. One day, everyone would forget what happened and things would go back to normal.'

Cason looked at his brother and began crying.
'No Billy, things aren't going back to normal!! I ruined my life. Everyone knows about this. No one can look at me the same. I just made a mistake Billy. I'm not a bad guy. But everyone thinks I am a bad guy!!'

He broke down and began crying.
Billy came by his brother and put his hand on Cason's back. The 2 were not affectionate by any means, so this was saying something.

Billy rubbed on Cason's back and began giving him some encouragement.

'Look Cason, we all make mistakes. It'll be okay. Nothing is going to happen to you. In a few months, everyone will forget about this. You'll get another job, and everything will be back to normal. Okay?'

Billy was saying the words, but inside, he felt like crying too. He knew Cason so well.

Cason was shy, introverted, and would often be asked to repeat himself when he spoke. Now seeing how all these strangers viewed him as some sort of party animal who was an alcoholic was killing Billy.
Especially because it was Billy who convinced Cason to go out in the first place.

Cason begrudgingly listened to his extroverted brother.

Where Cason was lowkey and quiet, Billy filled the room. He was the one who should have been caught on a show that covered DUI's. Billy lost count of how many times he had one too many to drink and got on the road. Each time, he made it home safe.

Seeing his little brother in such a shocking state, made him feel queasy. Billy couldn't sleep and his body felt like it was stuck in panic mode. Sweating, waking up from nightmares, and wondering if Cason really did ruin his life.

Cason was the normal one in the family.
Where all the other family members had big dreams and goals, Cason was the one who always wanted an ordinary life.

'Cason, look... You can sit down and keep crying or do something about this,' said Billy.

'What am I going to do? You don't know what I'm going through. I ruined my fucking life!! I went to get chocolate milk from 7/11 yesterday and the clerk asked me if I was the guy from the show.'

Cason felt rage at those producers for blatantly lying to him. He was not the kind of guy to feel immense rage, but this feeling was something that couldn't escape his body.
Because of those idiots, my life is ruined. What the fuck am I going to do now? I will get them back, he thought.

What was he going to do?

His house was dark for the next few months. Although the members in the house talked, there was an elephant in the room.

Cason was fired from his job.
Unsure what to do with his career.
And suffering from emotional breakdowns when he least expected it.

2

15 books.
These 15 books ranged from fiction to nonfiction.

Despite the dark times, Cason found one refuge. The refuge was in reading. When he would read, he would feel like the nightmare finally ended.

It's strange how he began enjoying books as of late. One part of that was because of the trauma of television. The DUI Dummies show was enough for him to have a disdain towards television.

He wasn't much of a radio guy. So, for him to kill time, he was reading more. Growing up, he hated reading. He hated reading and writing to be exact.

Cason had this teacher named Ms. Charnok growing up. She was this elderly lady in her mid-70s who would always lose his homework. He'd work on essays, expository and narrative included.

He was expecting an A+ to only see that she gave him an F for not having done the assignment.

'Ms. Charnok, I turned in the assignment. What are you talking about?'

Ms. Charnok looked back in disgust.

'Let me guess. You turned it in, but it magically got up and flew away. Is that what you expect me to believe?'

'No, I actually did the essays. I don't know why you don't have it.

Then Ms. Charnok proceeded to give him an F. The only way that Cason would pass the class was if he dominated the tests, quizzes, and group projects like a superstar. Since there was so much pressure to do well in those other fields, he felt a level of disgust working with language arts. Enough to hate reading.

Now, to kill time, he was finding ways to calm himself with the same books he was forced to read in school.

Lord of the Flies.
To Kill a Mockingbird.
I Know Why the Caged Bird Sings.

Cason wasn't too old, just 25. But he did notice that with some more life experience, he was able to resonate more with these books. Especially, To Kill a Mockingbird.

In the book, there was a man named Atticus Finch who was a reserved man. He was the father to a daughter named Scout and a son named Jem.

Atticus was assigned one of the most controversial cases in his town. He was assigned to represent a black man who was being accused of rape. The story of To Kill a Mockingbird was set in the era where racism was normal.

This case was enough to ruin Atticus's life. It was a lose-lose situation. If he won, then he won defending a black man against a white girl. If he lost, then he failed at defending a black man against a white girl.

Due to the era, any accusation against a black man was often seen as a death sentence for the black man.

Throughout the story, Atticus's children felt the effects of the high-profile case. Their classmates began insulting them. Atticus's own sister even said that he was bringing disgrace to the family.

Regardless, Atticus pushed forward.

That's what Cason felt he should be doing now.

Just push forward.

He loved reading nonfiction books on finance, social skills, accounting etc. But something about fiction books spoke to him.

It's as though he forgot about the travesty he was involved in, and he could teleport to a brand-new world. He continued to fly through the pages as he sat on the floor and leaned on his bed.

Page by page, the outdoors got darker and darker.

He turned the light on and read more pages.

3

Cason realized he needed to move out. This was probably the last thing that his parents were expecting.

'What do you mean you are going to move out, son? Look, I know you made a mistake, but we will get through this. We aren't kicking you out of the house. We want you to be okay,' said his father.

Cason wasn't having it.
It had been 4 months since the DUI.
At this point, he accepted what had happened. There was not much that he could do.

Within the past 4 months, Cason realized that he had been living life too safe. When he looked at the mirror, he even saw a safe look. No wow factor or anything.

Short hair, nothing too noticeable.
Average collared shirt, nothing too noticeable.
And average Levi's pants, nothing too noticeable.

From his internal world to external world, everything was predictable and routine. This recent terror shook up his internal world and there was a bitter attitude he was operating with.

Even though he didn't blame his parents or his brother, Cason wanted a change of scene from them. He needed to move out of Virginia.

Everyone in this town knew each other. Massive houses. It was reported that the side of Virginia he was in was one of the richest parts in all of the US. That's what repulsed Cason even more about this situation.

He felt like his brother and his parents put in their dues to earn such an amazing lifestyle. But Cason didn't do anything to deserve what he had.

'I know, dad. I want to say thank you so much for not kicking me while I'm down.'

Cason had been crying a lot.
It wasn't too much about the DUI Dummies show anymore.

It was a blend of 2 things:

1. How quickly his so-called friends turned on him.
2. And how his parents and his brother never wavered in their loyalty.

1 led to 2 being even more emotional for Cason.

He really felt like he had the best family in the world, and he felt like he didn't deserve it. Especially knowing how they had been suffering because of his mistake. How long they would suffer, he had no clue. All he knew was that he needed a change of scenery.

'Well, where are you going to live?'
'I don't know dad.'

'Then?'
'Well dad, I want to travel first.'

'Travel where?'
'I don't know dad.'

'Cason, look. I know what's happening. You made a mistake and want things to change bad. That's okay. But making rash decisions without any plans was never your thing. What you need to do now is get a job and start putting your life back together, not randomly traveling.'

'I know dad, you are right. The thing is, I'm not going to be a good hire for any company at the moment. I just need things to die down just a little. More importantly, I need to find myself.'

'What do you mean, Cason?'

'I need to find myself, dad. I realized after this whole ordeal that I'm not really a person. I'm just a collection of random ideas that I adopted to make other people happy. I have no fashion sense, no unique thoughts, no identity. All I do is live in a way to make others happy. I'm not really anyone, dad.'

'You are a great son and a great bother. Think like that. Don't focus so much on what is missing.'

'Dad, I know what you are saying, but I need you to also know what I'm saying. You are **that** guy....'

'What do you mean?'

'I mean, you are Enzo Enclosed. There is a brand presence to your name, dad. When others think of you, they think something. They think class, a winner, and a person who is articulate. When they think Cason, they think nothing.'

'Well, son. I got like this because I dedicated years to reading, studying, and working my way up. If you planted your feet in the ground, then you can make some sort of splash in accounting as well.'

Eh...accounting.
That phrase repulsed Cason.

That's something else that Cason did to be a people pleaser. His teacher asked him what he wanted to be growing up and he said he didn't know. So, his teacher said:
'You look like you will become an accountant one day.'

Just like that, Cason took those words as law. He never even questioned the teacher!
Just like a dummy, he said:
'I guess I will be an accountant.'

Then he organized his entire life around that 1 ideal. That ideal was never his. He liked accounting, but it was far from something he loved. Every day felt the same. Number crunching and little picture thinking.

Cason also found out that Billy was gifted with numbers. But his fit with numbers was much different than Cason. Billy was gifted with numbers by understanding and building businesses.

Billy looked like an average guy.
But he was becoming a mogul in the making.
He owned online brands that fed off one another. One brand would promote another brand and his profits would keep multiplying.

Billy learned how to play with numbers by creating value and then seeing how to increase his revenue and cut his costs.

2 simple steps:
- Increase revenue and cut costs.

What an elegant way to understand accounting and the numbers that Cason worked with. That level of simplicity only made Cason feel small.

He felt big when he was number crunching, memorizing all these random formulas and laws. Now, he was finally understanding the BIG picture view of what the hell he was routinely working on.

Just like Cason hated the television since the DUI Dummies show, he hated accounting because it reminded him of what a people pleaser he was.

'No dad, I need to do something bigger. I need to travel and discover myself.'

Enzo looked at his son with suspicion. He observed Cason, the good boy who never got in trouble suddenly getting into a whirlwind of trouble. Sure, he could try to stop his son from traveling, but then he would only be repeating the same mistake his dad made.

Enzo's dad never wanted him to become lawyer. He thought that was a disgraceful job that did society a lot of harm. He wanted Enzo to either be a doctor or an engineer. Those were safe jobs that would not involve being a disgrace. But Enzo decided that law was what he wanted to do.

He had a knack for breaking apart criminal cases and articulating himself with charm and conviction. When his father found out that he was going to pursue law, his father didn't talk to him for 15 years. His father didn't even come to his son's wedding.

The cold war finally ended when Enzo's father was going to pass away from lung cancer. He apologized to Enzo for how he treated him and wanted Enzo to be a better father to Cason and Billy.

Enzo already knew that he was going to support Cason. 'Alright son, do you need money?'

'I do.'

'How much?'

'How much can you give me?'

'How much do you need?'

'5000$?'

'Okay, I'll write you a check. Let's go, your mom is done with dinner.'

4

Cason had an idea where he was going to go.

He was going to go to Mexico.
Cozumel to be exact.

He had no clue why he wanted to go to Cozumel. That was a part of Mexico he had never heard of before. He was going through different cruise sites for inspiration.

Common places that tourists often go on cruises for are Jamaica, Bahamas, and Cozumel.

Hmm...Bahamas. That didn't sound bad.
Did they have TVs in Bahamas?

Even though Cason wasn't saying it out loud, he wanted to go to a place where they wouldn't recognize him. Seeing multiple people whisper and lower their voice when they walked past him had been traumatizing.

Cason walked downstairs and heard heels walking.
That's his mom.
He walks towards his mom with his book.

'Hey mom, what's up?

Where Enzo's dad had done a good job trying to hide his worries, mom was the opposite. She was visibly worried about Cason and would often express it.

'Hi, son. You okay? How are you feeling? You must feel awful, right?'

'Yea, I'm not feeling too good. Just taking it one day at a time.'

'Your dad says that you are planning on moving out and doing some traveling?'

'Yes, mom. I am.'

'You sure that's a good idea right now? Don't you think it would be better to stay here and get your life sorted out? I don't think you understand what a big deal this is, Cason. Not a great time to just get up and leave all your problems behind.'

Cason felt a gut punch in his stomach.
He knew that's exactly what it looked like. It seemed like he was just running away. But it was more than that.
He really was not running away, something in his gut told him that he **needed** to leave.

Cason didn't feel like he could talk to his mom about this. Where his father had a lot of tension with his dad before, Cason wasn't aware of any problems his mom faced. She probably did face some problems, but she was rarely vocal about it.

When Cason would ask about her life growing up, she'd only talk about the good parts. When Cason would ask about her day nowadays, she'd do the same thing and just talk about the good days.

The last person who was going to understand a trip like this would be his mom. Or at least, that's what he thought.

'I know what it looks like, mom. That I'm running away. But it's not like that. It's just that I haven't figured out who I am. I just need some time. I'm not like you where I always had things figured out.'

'What makes you think that I always had things figured out, Cason?'

'Didn't you?'

'No. No one ever has everything figured out. Every person out there is a work in progress. They are learning and doing the best they can, you hear?'

'Yes, I hear. But what do you mean you didn't have it figured out? I mean you did very well for yourself. Wasn't it always like that?'

'No, son. I didn't know much growing up about the fashion industry. I was actually a tomboy. Would act like my brothers. It was your grandma who scolded me and would often try to get me to hang out with her friends. Your grandma was very lady like. She was the one who was always wearing dresses.'

The last 2 words were important:
Wearing Dresses.

That was the name of Michelle's company. Her brand appealed to the exact opposite of tomboys. It was meant for feminine women or women who were trying to reconnect with their femininity.

As of late, a lot of the media was anti femininity. With the rise of female liberation, the whole idea of wearing dresses, being a housewife or anything traditional was seen as outdated and oppressive to women.

When Cason's mom first started her business, she was met with a flurry of backlash. Local news organizations thought she was not progressive enough and was trying to set the culture back. However, she still pushed on.

She continued to create new designs for her dresses and expanded from there. She went from dresses to makeup, and from makeup to perfume. Slowly, she was blossoming her empire 1 design at a time.

Soon, the media backlash turned into favorable coverage. They viewed Cason's mom as a modern-day Martha Stewart.

She was one of the few people who was doing what she was doing. Where a lot of other women's fashion brands were going out of their way to create pants and more boyish clothing, his mom was embracing femininity.

That's why it came as a shock when he learned that his mom never liked dresses in the first place.

'Wait!! Grandma made you wear dresses? You are the founder of Wearing Dresses!! What do you mean she made you?'

Cason's mom smirked.
'She made me, son. Initially, I hated the idea of socializing with all her friends. All they did was gossip and talk bad about people. But after a few meetings, I started to see the appeal. Something about the dresses resonated with me. It served as a symbol.'

'A symbol for what?'

'It was a symbol for being yourself and embracing femininity. I don't sell objects; I sell a feeling. You never know what each experience will lead you to. I know right now you are going through dark clouds, but just keep pushing forward.'

This type of encouraging words was not the type of words his mom would normally say. Normally, she was the first person to be negative and worry.

'I see what you're saying, mom. That's why I need to take this trip. It's something I really need to do. Does that make sense?'

She was silent for a while.
Then she smiled.
'Yes son, it makes sense. Good luck.'

5

Cason changed his mind.
Cozumel would have to wait.
Bahamas would be the destination.

He had been doing some research on which place he should take his trip to, and the white sand and crystal-clear water of the Bahamas beaches was what sold him. Yep, it was going to be Bahamas.

Since the DUI Dummies incident, Cason's introverted nature had turned him even more introverted. He still replayed how he was fired out of the blue moon.

His manager called him into the office.
'Hey Cason, how are you doing?'

The manager's name was Samuel. A heavy Latin man that didn't have shred of muscle.

Cason responded by saying good.

Samuel wasted no time getting to the point.

'Look Cason, I'm sure you know why I am calling you here. There are certain things we cannot tolerate in this company. The whole ordeal of drunk driving goes against our company's principles. I'm sorry to say this, but your job is terminated.'

Cason was let go.

What kind of BS was this?
His entire life, he was sold on the dream of job security, and just like that, he was fired? Not too secure now.

Cason knew himself well enough to know that he didn't have the stomach for entrepreneurship. The idea of not having a safe paycheck coming in for a couple of months to a couple of years terrified him. He gave his brother and mom major props for investing 5 plus years into their respective businesses before they were able to consistently get paid. But Cason knew that lifestyle was not for him.

If that wasn't for him, then what the hell was for him??

He didn't like accounting.
Wasn't much of a technical guy.
Hated blood, so medicine was clearly out of the question.

All he enjoyed lately was reading.
But what was going to do...
Become a writer?

Ha!!

He looked at the pile of books he had gone through in the past few months. He marveled at how these writers were such rich storytellers. The stories were so rich that he often felt like he knew the characters. They were his friends.

Of course, Cason would never be able to write something like that. A writer had to go to school for writing. That was the only way....

Wait a minute.

What does that even me?

Cason never heard of a bachelor's degree in becoming an author. How were these authors born in the first place?

Cason loved reading, but the idea of becoming a writer whose writings would be read by others was a pipe dream.

A guy could dream nevertheless.
This trip to Bahamas would be something that would help spark some inspiration in him.

Hopefully.

6

Cason booked the trip. He was set to leave in 2 days.

Leading up to his trip, his parents and brother all sat at the table to have dinner.

Enzo broke the silence.
'Any idea how long you are going to be gone for, son?'

'Not sure yet, dad.'

It was clear that Cason's mom was not sold on this plan even though she had seemed encouraging. When she found out that Cason booked a 1-way trip, her worried face began to look even more worried.

Billy was supportive and gave Cason one piece of advice which would end up serving as a battle cry for Cason. The advice was simple, 3 words to be exact:
'Take strategic risks.'

Billy even took it a few levels further. 'When you try to avoid risks... that's the riskiest thing to do.'

Billy went onto tell Cason about a few lessons he learned since running a business. One of the lessons was that either you innovate or die. There is no such thing as maintaining for too long in business.

Innovation is born from experimenting, failing, and taking risks. That's one of the reasons that Billy ended up becoming so successful at such an early age.

Initially, it wasn't like that. He was failing and trying to be safe. When he would make a couple of dollars, he would keep trying to save that so he could rest on his laurels. But when he began taking strategic risks, that's when he felt fearless and fearful at the same time.

Within that polarity is when his business started to take off.

The advice resonated with Cason. There was the quote he once heard which said that *when you run away from problems, problems find you.*

Since he had been playing it safe his entire life, problems were bubbling in the backend. It's like we were put on this planet to get into problems and solve them. The type of problems that we willingly chose to solve would determine our success rates. No running away.

After dinner, Cason went back to his room to read some more. That's when Enzo came in.

'Got a minute, son?'

'Yes, dad. Whatsup?'

Enzo sat down.

'Just wanted to make sure you weren't going to do anything drastic in Bahamas.'

One second, one family member is telling him to take risks and the other family member is asking him not to do anything drastic?

'What do you mean, dad?'

'I just want to make sure you don't do anything to harm yourself. Like drugs, too much alcohol, or worse...'

'Oh no dad, it really isn't like that. I'm mainly doing this trip to see who I really am. I'm not going there to be a degenerate or anything. To be honest, I don't know if I will ever touch alcohol again. One of the rare few times I do it, I find myself on TV.'

Both father and son laugh.

'Okay son, if you're not going to do drugs, then that makes me feel good. Mind if I give you some advice?'

'Yea dad, whatsup?'

'Take strategic risks.'

What the heck??
Billy had just told him that.
Were Billy and dad talking?

'Were you talking to Billy about telling me that?'

'No, why?'

'Because Billy literally told me to take strategic risks too!!'

Enzo looked puzzled and began laughing at the coincidence, then continued.

'No, I didn't talk to Billy about giving you that advice. I guess it's just something you needed to hear. Look son, you said you want to find yourself, right?'

Cason nodded his head.

'Well, I want you to look around this world. It's just ideas everywhere. Ideas which we take as reality. The street lights, ideas. What is and what is not illegal, ideas. The money I'm holding? Ideas.'

Cason continued to listen.

'These ideas are other people's ideas that we are all in agreement on. And if you are agreeing too much, then you are just going to be a sum of someone else's ideas. That's why I'm telling you to take some strategic risks while you're there, son. I gave you 5000$. I hope you aren't living in Bahamas the same exact way you are leaving here.'

'What risks have you taken, dad?'

'Marrying your mom was one of them. I'm not going to lie, but I didn't want a career woman. I wanted a woman who was going to stay home and take care of the kids while I rose in my career. When I saw that your mom was just as serious about her career as I was about mine, it got me a little nervous.'

'Why?'

'I don't know. I think it's because my dad and mom had a traditional relationship and I just adopted the idea. The minute that it was being challenged, I didn't know what to do next.'

'So, what did you do?'

'At first, I got scared. I told your mom that I would have to leave her if she didn't push her career to the side. Your mom did not agree to my demands. However, she still wanted to make it work.'

Enzo paused to see if Cason was not bored.
He wasn't.
Enzo continued.

'I had a bunch of friends who told me to break up with your mom. They had bad experiences with career women, and they would tell me to get out while I still could. My father and friends said that career women were not worth it. But I had to listen to my gut. I took a strategic risk. I weighed all the experience I had with your mom, her actions, and realized that it was a risk worth taking. If it didn't work out, then it didn't work out. But if it did work out, then I would be grateful.'

'What did you learn?'

'I learned that not all advice is good advice. Because others are giving advice from their point of view. What works for one person may not work for another person. If I listened to my dad and my friends, then I wouldn't be having this conversation with you right now. See... that's where Billy and you have always been different.'

'How have we been different?'

'Billy was the troublemaker growing up. I used to worry about him a lot. Thought he was going to go to jail or do something reckless. But he was a troublemaker in the school's standards. What I realized later as a parent was that Billy wasn't the problem, it was the school system's problem. Actually, both were in the wrong. It's just that Billy didn't have the personality type to be sitting in class. That's where you were different.'

Cason began to think about their childhood. Billy would get suspended, get into fights and stack up referrals like Pokémon cards. While Cason was often loved by the teachers. Better yet, he was ignored by the teachers. They'd often forget his name because he was so much of a background type of guy.

'Cason, your mom and I liked what a good boy you were growing up. You still are a good boy. But we felt like we robbed you off that fearlessness at an early age. That fearlessness is a muscle, son. A part of me feels like I'm to blame for your identity crisis right now.'

'No dad, you're not to blame at all! You've been great through this entire process. I feel so bad about how I let you down. I'm going on this trip not to show what bad parents you were, but because of what a bad son I was. I want to change that.'

Enzo smiled hearing the positive acknowledgment.

'I see what you're saying, son. Just realize that taking risks is not a bad thing in life. It's a part of life. Those who refuse to take risks adopt other people's ideas and call them their own. Then one day, they wonder why they feel empty. I don't want you to feel empty.'

'Do you enjoy what you do for a living, dad?'

'Yes son, it's my life. I don't work, I perform my calling every day. Think like that. Calling.'

'I mean it's just words, what's the big deal?'

'A job is something you have to do. A calling is something that you are called to do. It's a night and day difference. Growing up, I used to watch a lot of movies and clips on law. I was highly curious about the criminal justice system. I also wanted to know how logic, words, and evidence could be used to sway someone's life for the best or the worst. I loved everything about law. Your calling is often a thing that you consume the most.'

'What do you mean?'

'Look at your mom for example. She was obsessed with dresses as long as I could remember. She'd be able to dissect the material, the dress size, whether the supplier was competent or not. She would routinely consume dress magazines, dress videos and all sort of fashion content. That's why what she does comes easy to her.'

'Hm...that's really interesting.'

'Look at Billy. When I'd walk around with him in the streets growing up, he would explain why certain businesses worked and why some didn't. At the age of 7, he was reverse engineering pizza places, business plans, product development and all of that! What do you like to consume?'

'As of late dad, I've been reading a lot more.'

'Why?'

'I have no clue. Well…. I think I sort of have a clue. It was because I am somewhat scared with the TV. I don't know if I can watch one of those for some time.'

'Are you reading because you despise the TV or are you reading because you actually love reading?'

'A little bit of both. As of late, I've been loving books. It's the only thing that makes me forget about this nightmare.'

'What do you read?'

'I read self-improvement books, autobiographies, and fiction.'

'Fiction, huh?'
'Yes. I've been reading fiction and dad, I think I know what you're talking about with the calling thing. I wouldn't say I'm going to be a writer or anything. But something about writing **captivates** me. It's like I can create this alternate universe for the reader to temporarily enter.'

Cason had more things to say, but he was getting a bit emotional. He continued nevertheless.

'These past months have been hell, dad. I walk down the streets and others are talking about me. I hear this internet thing is only going to get more advanced in the years. Soon, more people are going to consume more stuff from the internet than the TV. I'm sure my episode of DUI Dummies is going to be on that YouTube thingy. I'm sure people are going to see me at the lowest point of my life and think that's who I am....'

Enzo was about to interrupt, but he decided not to. So, Cason continued.

'These books, dad. It allows me to enter a different universe and ....feel.... feel good again, do you know what I mean?'

'I've never been much of a fiction reader, but I get your point.'

'Something about writing has been captivating me as of late. I wish I could put it into words. Some of these authors are really good. They write in a way where it's so simple to understand! Anyways, I'm just talking out loud. I don't know what I'm going to do with writing. Just you bringing up finding a calling and talking about looking into what I consume the most has got me thinking, you know?'
'I know son, I know. Just keep brainstorming. Experiment more. I know this Bahamas trip is going to help you out more than you can imagine.'

'Thanks, dad.'

7

Getting to Bahamas was a pretty chilling experience for Cason. This was probably one of the riskiest things he ever did. Well, besides getting behind the wheel while he was drunk.

Now he was in Bahamas, with little clue what to do next.

He had money, so he could get a hotel.
Well, how long was he going to stay?
Should he get an apartment instead?

No, start off with a hotel and then see if an apartment would be better.

He called the taxi driver and asked the driver to take him to a nearby hotel.
The driver dropped him off in a dingy motel that didn't look safe to visit. Oh well, he decided to go there anyway.

Cason got his 1 suitcase and back pack and was greeted by a tan woman with a pretty face.
'Hello there sir, how are you?'

'I'm doing well, miss. Can I get 1 room please?'

'Sure, for how long?'

'Can it be undetermined?'

'I'm going to need a date to enter into the system, sir.'

'Let's say 1 week.'

Cason had a feeling it was going to be longer than 1 week.

The lady got him acclimated.

He was wearing a cap and glasses to hide his face just in case she recognized him from the show. He desperately hoped that she didn't break the silence with:
'Hey, aren't you the guy from....'

He lost track of how many times he was asked that question since the premiere of the show. It was embarrassing because anytime he had an interaction with someone new, in the back of his mind, he was carrying himself like he was about to be asked the question.

Luckily, she didn't ask him anything like that. She nevertheless had some questions for Cason.

'What's your story, mister?'

'Huh?'

'Like... what's your story?'

Cason didn't know what the hell she was asking. Was this her subvert way of asking about his television appearance? Since she didn't blatantly ask the question, he'd just answer in an equally vague way.

'I'm just trying to find myself, you know?'

She looked back at him.
Her face was very small, with big lips and long hair. She was cute. The way her face was structured, she seemed like someone who did a lot of probing.

'I see what you're saying....' she looked at his driver's license '...Cason.'

Cason nodded and got his motel keys.

As he was walking to his room, he became angry.

He thought:
Dammit, you idiot! She was trying to create conversation with you. You should have said something to keep the conversation going!! You're supposed to take some risks in this trip, dummy.

He angrily walked into the room. Nothing special. Tiny room, tiny bed, and no TV. Thank God for the no TV part.

His motel room was on the second floor. Once he opened the window, he saw an amazing view of the beach.

Great, a nice beach, he thought.
Time to walk around and take some strategic risks...

8

Cason walked around the area. He saw different locals talking to one another.
He walked some more.
Then he saw tourists.

He walked some more...
Now he had locals coming to sell him something like he was a tourist.

Didn't they know that he was going to be one of the locals too?

'Sir! May I interest you in this?'

A tiny shriveled up woman comes to him holding a black tank top with Bob Marley's face on it.

Cason looked back at the tank top, it did look nice.
'Um...how much?'

'20 dollars,' said the woman.

20 dollars?? Cason thought.

The shirt was nice, but 20 dollars? He was hesitant to buy any clothes that weren't on a deal. His shirts were often in the $12.99 mark. Anything more than that was inspected thoroughly.

As his analytical mind began creeping up while he was feeling on the shirt, that's when he heard his brother and father's words:
'Take strategic risks.'

He thought:
Well, what the hell does strategic mean in the first place? Does me buying this Bob Marley shirt count as strategic or not?

He began thinking and thinking some more. Clearly his face must have looked strange since he was thinking so much that the shriveled woman broke the silence.

'You're a skinny boy. You need to eat more.'

Wow, what a great saleswoman.

'Um yea...this is my first day here. Do you have any idea where I should eat?'

That's when the shrivel woman looked at him in shock. Suddenly, her motherly instincts took over.
'Wait, you haven't eaten yet? It's almost dark!'

'No miss, I have not eaten yet.'

'Okay young man, I'll make you a deal. If you buy this Bob Marley shirt, then I will make you food. It's a 1 time offer that will expire in 40 seconds.'

Suddenly, Cason felt pressure.

He began to have a flurry of questions.
- When the hell am I ever going to wear this Bob Marley shirt?
- Who the hell is this lady and what if she is trying to poison me??
- What if her food sucks???

As time was winding down, she begins counting down.
'10..

9..

8.'

Think Cason, think!!

'7...

6..

5..

4..'

Cason made up his mind.

'Okay, deal!'

The shriveled-up woman gave him the shirt for the money and began walking Cason back to a certain location. He had no clue where she was taking him.

What if she was setting him up so she could get the Bob Marley shirt back?

Even though he was uncertain, he felt good right now.

Billy and his dad told him to take strategic risks and when he thought about it, he felt like buying the shirt was his first strategic risk.

Something about risks always terrified Cason.
One of the earlier times he recalled taking a risk and it backfiring was when he snitched on a classmate.

He was in music class as a kid.

There was a teacher who saw one of her flutes were stolen. She said the entire class would get an F on the project if none of the students said who took the item.

All the kids in the class knew who took it.
It was a kid named James who was notorious for stealing things and fighting others.

The other kids didn't say a word.

Cason thought it was worth the risk to snitch on James. He was sure he would get on the teacher's good side and win the approval of his classmates.

Once he told on James, he felt a strong slap on the back of his head.

He turned around and it was James ferociously looking at him. The other classmates also disapprovingly looked at him. They couldn't believe that he snitched on James so quickly.

After that, not only did he lose a bunch friends, he also lost the stomach to take risks. That was such a subtle memory. It happened when he was 7ish.

But they often say that a significant part of childhood determines adulthood. That memory from 7-year-old may have been forgotten by the conscious mind, but it sure as hell wasn't forgotten by the subconscious mind.

'Um... how much longer do we have miss?'

He looked at the tiny woman as she was walking with purpose. Something about someone her age walking with such a strong stride seemed abnormal.

'We're almost there. What's your name?'

'My name is Cason. Yours?'

'They call me Auntie.'

'Who calls you Auntie? What's your real name?'

The shriveled woman looks back at Cason.
'I prefer you call me Auntie.'

Cason thought, Auntie?? Why would he call a random woman he just met Auntie? That didn't make any sense. Oh well, she was going to be feeding him so he wasn't going to ask any questions.

Finally, the lady begins heading into a neighborhood where all the houses were different colors.

Pink, purple, yellow.

Even though the houses looked raggedy, the different colors made them pop.

She pulls up to the pink house and opens the door.
The lights are on.
Cason could hear a buzzing of voices and the smell was amazing. He didn't know what the smell was, all he knew was that it was food.

His stomach was growling, and his mouth was getting dry.

'Take your shoes off, young man. I will introduce you to everyone.'

As he begins taking his shoes off, he hears a loud:
'Auntie!!!!'

2 little girls come rushing towards her.
'Hi there, my 2 little angels!!'

The two girls hug Auntie and look at Cason with curiosity.

Auntie quickly introduces both parties.
'Hello Cason, this is Reene and Shiv. Reene and Shiv, this is Cason.'

The 2 girls lunge towards him and give him a hug. Surprised, Cason begins laughing and they begin hugging him tighter.
'Nice to meet you 2 girls!'

Auntie looks at Cason and says, 'let me introduce you to the others.

That's when the strong food smell gets even stronger.

He walks into a kitchen that has at least 12 people. How the hell are all these people fitting in this tiny house??

They all yell out:
'Auntie!! We've been waiting for you.'

Then they see Cason sneaking up behind her. A few people look suspiciously while the others realized it must be Auntie being social.

'Hey everyone., I have a guest who will be joining us for dinner. Everyone, say hello to Cason!'

'Hi Cason!!' everyone said in unison.

Cason got nervous. He wasn't used to seeing all these eyeballs looking at him.

'Um… hi,' he said without a semblance of charm.

Auntie pulled up an extra plate and a chair for Cason to sit down. A few of the people went back to talking about what they were talking about before while a few other members began talking to Cason.

One elderly man who looked roughly around the same age as Auntie was one of the first people to break ice with Cason.

'So, what bought you to Bahamas of all places?'

Soon as the elderly man spoke, everyone else quieted down. Now the table was looking at Cason.

While the table was looking at Cason, Auntie was assembling Cason's turkey, mashed potatoes, corn, and extra meatloaf.

'Um...I saw a lot of the beaches and I had to come.'

The table began laughing.

The 2 girls who initially greeted Cason were like:
'You'll love the beaches!'

The old man smiled and continued to probe.
'You came here only for the beaches? No. I can tell you didn't come for vacation. Why did you really come? Running away from something?' he asked.

When he asked that, Cason suddenly got nervous.
Oh no, does he know about the TV show?

Cason didn't want to be weird, so he quickly said:
'No sir, I'm not running away. Actually, I'm trying to find myself.'

This was a compelling answer that the table was not expecting. There was another boy who was roughly around Cason's age who asked:
'That's interesting. So, this is like a spiritual trip, huh?'

'I would say so. Even though I'm not too much of a spiritual guy. For me, I just have been feeling lost as of late. I don't know who I am. I thought it would be best if I took some time away from life and be alone to discover who I am.'

That's when the old man smirked, gathered his thoughts and said:
'You don't find yourself away from life. You find yourself while getting your ass kicked by life.'

Auntie looked at the old man and angrily said:
'Hey, we don't use bad words!'

The old man smiled.

'What do you mean, sir?' Cason asked.

'People often come to Bahamas as a tourist. They have a lot of stress in their 40 hour a week jobs, relationships, and life in general. So, they come here to escape and relax. Which they do. The only problem is that when they go back to where they came from, they just go back to feeling stressed again.

Auntie gave Cason his plate.

'I believe you are smart. What's your name?'

'Cason, yours?'

'You can call me Uncle.'

Uncle?? Now Cason was becoming confused. One person goes by Auntie and the other person goes by Uncle. Was this some kind of tradition in Bahamas or were these 2 people pulling his leg?!

'Look Cason, you have a great opportunity. People who come to Bahamas need to experience this place the right way. You hang with this family and we will teach you to experience it the right way. We can challenge you and kick your ass some more!'

Once again, Auntie got angry:
'Hey!! Stop saying that word!!'

Uncle smiled.
Cason had no clue what he meant.

'What do you do, Uncle?' Cason asked.

That's when the bunch of people in the table looked around stunned as if the question was insulting.

The guy who was Cason's age said:
'Uncle is the celebrity in this house. The reason we always have food on the table is because of him.'

Cason looked at Uncle with curiosity.

Uncle pulled out a pen from his right front pocket.
'This has made me a lot of money,' Uncle said as he waved the pen in front of Cason.

'A pen, sir?'

'Oh oops, I forgot the other part. A paper... But yes, the pen has made me a lot of money.'

One of the little girls interrupted:
'Our uncle is a good writer. A lot of people from America come to get training from him. He's a writer of so many books!'

Wait, he's a writer?
Cason had his first question.

'Um Uncle...which school did you go to learn writing? Is the school here?'

The table burst out laughing.

Auntie said:
'School?? Haha!!'

The table began laughing at Cason's suggestion that Uncle learned how to write in school.

Uncle responded.
'School doesn't teach you how to write. Life teaches you how to write. If you want, I can teach you to write.'

'Teach me? You will do that?'

'Yea, if you let me kick your ass some more.'

'Hey!!' Auntie screamed again.

Cason was confused.
'Sir?'
'Great writers are born from pain. Are you okay with welcoming pain?'

'Uh... I guess.'

'Okay, then you will become a great writer. Writing skills are born from not only welcoming pain, but organizing it into knowledge and then communicating the knowledge.'

One of the members from the table said:
'Uncle is one of the famous writers in the Bahamas. He makes it easy to learn. Others get bogged down with too much little details.'

Uncle continued.
'Anyways, I want you and Ivan to start shadowing me. This old man needs something fun to do!'

'Ivan?'

'That's me.'

Cason looked at the other kid who was roughly around his age.

Cason didn't know why but be began feeling excited. First day in Bahamas and he was already getting acclimated with the area. He had his Bob Marley shirt, met a few people, and now got his writing mentor.

What could possibly make this first day even better??

This was going to be the beginning of a new chapter.

He desperately hoped that these fine people were not made aware of his appearance on the television show.

Everything was going so well too...

9

Cason spent the night chatting with the people in the house and exchanging stories. A lot of them were curious what the US was like… not like Bahamas was too far from the US. But the people in the house were locals who never left Bahamas.

Cason described the good parts of the US along with the bad sides and they listened to his words with curiosity. He was surprised how easy it was sharing these stories. For the most part, he was normally a bad storyteller. However, this group made him feel comfortable. It's like they were just waiting to hear his words with enthusiasm.

As Auntie prepared dessert, Cason found himself being more animated than usual. He was using wide hand gestures, changing his tonality, and moving his body around. There were a few times he told jokes that had the entire audience laughing.

Anytime he'd get done telling his stories, Uncle would look at him and say:
'You're going to make a great writer. Great speakers become great writers.'

Cason looked at him confused.

Great speaker?
Who the hell was this old man speaking to??

Hearing that little bit of encouragement did a lot for his confidence. Normally, he was reserved and to himself. However, since being in Bahamas, he was already starting to feel like a brand-new person.

Maybe this strategic risk concept was not so bad after all. He had to find a job while he was at Bahamas. Why not ask someone here?

'By the way folks, I have a favor to ask.'

The room hushes.
'What is it?' Auntie asks.

'I need a job. Do you know anyone who is hiring?'

The room began chatting.
There was a woman who was roughly in her mid-40s who said:
'I could use some help.'

Ivan got up and said:
'That's my mom. She owns one of the best sandwich shops in the entire Bahamas.'

The woman looked at him funny.
'*One* of the best sandwich shops? It is the best sandwich shop! Since Ivan is too lazy to help me, why don't you help me? I will pay you every week.'

Hm...sandwich shop.

Cason was an accountant not too long ago. Wouldn't making sandwiches for a living out of nowhere seem like a downgrade?

Wait.

Who was he kidding?
His life as of late had been a downgrade, he had no room to be picky.

'I would love to make sandwiches with you. When can I begin?'

'How about tomorrow?'

Uncle was observing Cason as he was accepting the job role. That's when he looks at Ivan and says:
'Ivan, I want you to work in the sandwich shop with Cason as well.'

'What, why??' Ivan asked surprised.

'Because since I am going to be teaching you 2 writing, I want you 2 to get familiar with each other. People often learn faster when they talk to others about what they learned. I think it would help if you guys can bounce ideas of one another.'

'Okay, sure.'

Ivan was happy as well. Before, he hated working at the sandwich shop because his mom was a micromanager and he had no one else to talk to. But if this new funny kid named Cason was going to be working with him, then it would be easier to kill time.

Ivan had a dream of being a great writer like his Uncle. The way that his uncle was able to turn complex topics into poetry captivated him. He also had dreams of working on his own schedule. Ivan loved his mom but the idea of working at a sandwich shop forever didn't appeal to him at all. If he was able to become a better writer and build an audience along the way, then it would be a great opportunity to level up towards his dreams.

Cason looked at Ivan.
Ivan looked at Cason.

They knew within the next couple of days, weeks or months... they'd be getting to know each other very well.

10

'You are coming back late.'

Cason looked back as the cute hostess greeting him. He looked at the clock and it showed 12 am.

Cason looked back at the hostess and saw her name, Brooke, on the name tag. He said:
'Yes, let's just say I met an interesting group of people. You are working late.'

'Well, I'm working late because tonight is my last night.'

Cason was taken aback. Last night? He was hoping to have some more interactions with this attractive hostess.

'Wait, really?? Where are you moving?'

'Oh, I'm not moving. I just got a different job. My mom needs some help in her hotel and asked if I'd be willing to help.'

'You love the hotel and motel business, huh?' Cason asked with a smirk.

'Haha, that's what it must look like. Not really, I actually always wanted to be an actress. But times are tough and it seems like I'm always getting caught up in different jobs to make ends meet, you know?'

She asked him a question back. That meant she wanted the conversation to go on.

Strategic risks.

Those 2 words came ringing in Cason's mind again. He was wondering if he should ask her on a date.

You know what?? Fuck it.

'Um. You seem very interesting. I'd love to get to know you more. Any chance you'd want to go on a date sometimes?'

Brooke's smile turned into a frown.
'Um... I'm so sorry, but I'm in a relationship.'

Then she pointed at a picture behind her where she was being held by a tall handsome guy.

Embarrassed, Cason looked for a quick way to rebound.
'Oh yea, but who couldn't use 2 boyfriends? Just kidding.'

She pulled out a piece of paper and began writing something down.

'Here. This is my number if you ever need me. I know you are new to Bahamas, but I've been here my entire life. Text me or call me if you ever have any questions.'

This was still a win in Cason's mind. Even though he didn't get the date, he at least got her number. Knowing how clumsy he could get with his phone, he decided to get a piece of paper and write down his number too.

'For sure, Brooke. I wish you the best in your new job. If you ever need me, this is my number. Don't hesitate to reach out.'

He said the last sentence with a lot of force as if reinforcing: 'Seriously, do not hesitate.'

They both waved each other goodbye, and he began walking to his room.

As he lied down, he felt a thrill.
This was a thrill that he hadn't felt in ages.

Billy and dad were right. This strategic risks thing was way better than he was initially expecting. Cason was saddened that it took him so long to figure this out.

'I'm going to be taking a lot more risks while im here. I'll be a changed person once I leave Bahamas. That's a promise.'

11

'Listen Cason, you are not just a sandwich maker. You are a sandwich artist. Say it with me, I am a sandwich artist.'

'I am a sandwich artist.'

This was Cason's first day on the job and he was already feeling a little doubtful. Ivan said his mom was a micromanager, but he wasn't expecting it to be so intense from the get-go.

Cason was only 2 minutes late on his first day, and he got an earful from his manager. She also expected Cason to call her 'maam.'

The job didn't feel too bad. He liked the idea of creating sandwiches from chaos.

He'd make subs.
Pitas.
And even salads.

One of the most gratifying feelings was when he made his first sub and the customer gave him a tip. Not only did she give him a tip, she came back once she was done with the meal and said:

'That was the best sandwich I've had in a long time. Bravo.'

Cason liked hearing that.
He had been a consumer for so long that he didn't now what it was like to be a creator. There was a different feeling in knowing that he was responsible for making this lady's day better.

The shop would get busy in spurts.
Sometimes, it would get so busy that he was working incessantly. He liked it when it was busy because that's when the day would fly right by. When it was empty, that's when it took a long time for the day to fly by.

When it was empty, he and Ivan would stock the supplies. They'd fill up the pickles, jalapenos, meats, and cheeses. Not only would they fill up the food trays, they would talk as well.

'Seriously though Cason, why are you here?'

'What do you mean?'

'I mean you seem like a normal guy. What makes a normal guy wake up one morning and say that he's going to be living in the Bahamas? Are you mad at your parents or something?'

'No. Actually dude, I have the 2 best parents out there. My dad is a renowned lawyer and my mom runs a successful business.'

'Then?'

'Why can't you believe that I just came here to explore the Bahamas?? Haha.'

'Listen Cason, Uncle wants us to get close because we are going to be seeing each other a lot for the next couple of weeks. Seriously, what happened? What are you running away from?'

'Okay Ivan, I'll tell you.'

Cason was going to tell Ivan something but he definitely was not going to tell him the entire story. There was no chance he was going to be jeopardizing what he was beginning to have here.

'Okay look, Ivan. I have always been this shadow everywhere I went. I didn't have much of an identity in the US. I worked an average job, dressed like an average guy, and didn't have many opinions that were my own.'

Ivan listened.

'So, I wanted to change that. I'm 25 years old and still have no clue who I really am. The one reason why is because I don't take any risks. My older brother told me that, as did my dad. So, I thought it would be risky coming to Bahamas where I didn't know anyone and start something here. I don't know exactly what I am looking for, but I'm sure I'll find something.'

Ivan was silent for a second, processing what he just heard.

'You know what Cason?'

'What?'

'Me and you are going to be very close.'

'Oh yea? Why do you say that?'

'It's because ever since my dad died...'

'Whoa, your dad died? I'm so sorry to hear about that man.'

'It's okay. Maybe one day you'll find out how he died. If you are open with me, then I'll be open with you. Anyways, ever since my dad died, I've been feeling off. My mom hasn't been the same. She's been having to work more. It feels like I've been getting pulled in all these different directions. My dream was to always work for myself. This sandwich making thing isn't bad, but I don't want to be here my entire life. I don't even know if I want to be in Bahamas my whole life. I feel like I have yet to see the world. I'm only 25 too. You've been in the US. You've seen what it's like. We all talk about going to the US in the Bahamas, but for us, that's a pipedream. I want to become a wordsmith so I can build an empire around me. Does that make sense?'

Surprisingly, Cason knew exactly what Ivan was talking about. Wow.... How random was it that the kid who he was going to be shadowing with had been so similar in terms of their mannerisms?

They both had big dreams.
They both felt unsure about what to do next.
And they both **knew** that writing was going to play some role in their future.

Still, Cason had no clue what to expect from these writing practices.

'Ivan, what can we expect from Uncle? You know him and you've worked with him. What should I expect?'

'Actually Cason, he strictly told me not to say anything to you. He wanted the first meeting to be a surprise.'

'What? Why? What happened to us being open with each other!' Cason said in a sarcastic tone.

'Hey man, I'd love to, but this is the one thing that Uncle told me to not tell you about. You'll see why.'

'Okay, I'll take your word for it.

As their conversation was winding down, they both saw a heavy woman waiting at the sandwich isle.
'What's a woman got to do to get a tuna sub around here!'

'You got her Ivan, or you want me to get her?'

'Hey, you're the sandwich artist,' Ivan said.

12

Cason came back to his hotel to get ready. His first meeting with Uncle was going to be in 2 hours. He thought it would be the perfect time to get a quick nap in, get changed, and walk over to the sandwich shop so Ivan could pick him up from there.

As he entered the hotel, he saw a guy in the same spot that Brooke used to be. He felt a subtle tug on his heart strings. He wished he had a longer time to get to know Brooke. She seemed like she could teach him some things.

He lied down.

Thus far, it had been a different scenario for him. He was not used to not being recognized in public.

Thus far, he had been someone who never wanted to be a celebrity. The only reason he became a celebrity was for all the wrong reasons.

He lied down on his bed feeling somewhat hopeful about the change his life was projecting towards. He already got a new job, a mentor, and a friend in his first few days in Bahamas. If he had the same shy attitude he had back in Virginia, he doubted he'd have left the hotel.

Cason knew that he was going to give this Bahamas thing a shot.

He lied down on the bed and dozed off.
As he began to doze off.... he began dreaming.
Better yet...he began having a **nightmare**....

'I don't know if I should take another one guys.'

His coworkers were not having it.

'Come on Cason, quit being a baby!! Hahaha just take it.'

'I seriously don't know if I should. I might throw up.'

'Cason, I ordered it for the entire team. Quit being a buzzkill. Come on guys, tell Cason to quit being a baby. Cason, Cason, Cason!!'

One of the waitresses heard what was being said.
She grabs Cason's shoulder and says
'Come on, quit being a baby! I was the one who made the pickle backs too.'

Peer pressure was at an all-time high.

Cason, who was normally seen as a recluse, was finally out with his coworkers. It was 4 other guys roughly around his age. They had been trying to get Cason to come out for the longest, but Cason always had some elaborate excuse.

This night, they were able to get Cason to come out because they promised Veronica was going to come too. She was one of the HR reps that Cason had a crush on. Everyone on the floor knew that he had a crush on her.

He didn't want to take the shot because he felt that Veronica was coming soon and he didn't want to talk to her with his speech slurring.

'I seriously can't guys.'

'Okay, if you don't take it, then none of us are taking it either.'

The others looked at him with a sad face.
That's when Cason said:
'Okay, fine. Last shot though!!'

Cason was okay with letting himself down. But whenever others felt like they were let down by him, he was not happy. He was a people pleaser to the core.

Cason picked up the shot, clinked it with the other shot glasses and they all took it in unison.

'Yea!!!!' Said one of the drunk members.

'Jake, shut up man! We are out in public. Haha. We know who definitely is not driving.'
At this point, Cason was more than tipsy.

He was drunk.

He asked:
'By the way, when is Veronica coming?'

That's when the other members began looking at each other. They were looking like, *who wants to break the news?*

Jake, the person who just got done screaming, broke the news.

'Yea Cason.... Veronica is not coming. We just said she was coming so you would finally come out of the cube.'

'What?? Are you serious?'

'Yea. Look, the place is about to close in 15 minutes. You think Veronica is really coming?'

The other members began laughing.
But Cason didn't find it funny at all.

He thought, *so he got this drunk for no reason? What the hell!*

Soon, the place had closed.
The other members walked out.
The thought of them driving drunk didn't come up at all. They effortlessly got in their cars and drove away.

Seeing how his coworkers didn't make it a big deal about driving drunk, he didn't think it was a big deal either. Sure, he heard a few times that it was not the smart thing to do, but what's the worst that could happen? It was only a 22-minute drive back home. Nothing bad could happen.

Only, something bad would happen.

When he was on the highway, it was empty for the most part. Then as he was 8 minutes away according to the GPS, he saw cop lights from his rearview mirror. His heart sank, but he didn't quite understand the weight of the situation.

The rest was history.

He was pulled out of the car after slurring his words.
Given a DUI test.

As he was doing the test, everything felt like a dream. It didn't feel like a real moment. Just a hazy occurrence.

As he was done, all he could remember was a guy in a suit coming out and telling him that he was going to be on TV. Still, Cason didn't understand the weight of the situation.

Until the next day when he recalled the experience. When he was in the jail house, he found a way to cover his tracks. He told his parents that he was going to be chilling with his coworkers for some time.

They believed him like they always did.
The only problem was that Cason knew his life was never going to be the same once he fully sobered up.

Cason suddenly woke up from the nightmare.

He was sweating.

This nightmare was replaying for a few months. It's like different angles of that night were still locked in his subconscious mind and every time he dreamt, he was given a new peak into what happened.

The host of the show was in the cop car the entire time, listening in on the conversation. He was waiting for the perfect time to let Cason know that he was going to be on TV.

As Cason recalled that memory, he slowly became infuriated.

His life was going well. Why was it that these idiots went out of their way to ruin it? Didn't they have anything better to do? If Cason ever had the resources, he was going to find that smug television host and spit on his face.

Then again though, the whole ordeal was Cason's fault.

Once Cason woke up, he kept dwelling on that night. He could feel his enthusiasm waning and now he wasn't even sure if he wanted to go to the training.

Then again, he had no choice.
He already gave Uncle and Ivan his word.

Cason slowed his breath down.
He forcefully put a smile on his face and began getting ready.

13

'You are late,' Ivan said as he was staring at his watch and back at Cason.

'What is with you and you mom? I'm just 2 minutes late and you guys make it a big deal?' Cason said in a joking way.

'Late is late, my friend. Let's go.'

Ivan got in his car with Cason and began driving off. The sun was setting, and it was getting dark. Ivan had a pretty worried look on his face.

Cason literary had no clue what to expect.
I thought I was supposed to be learning how to write. Why the hell are we driving late at night for? I wonder if something shady is going to happen.

After 40 minutes, they finally got to a dark park like area.
'Ivan, where the hell are we?'

Ivan begins reaching in his glove compartment. Then he pulls out a blindfold.
'Uncle told me to tell you to put this on.'

'What??? I'm definitely not wearing that. Why would I wear a blindfold? Quit joking around and lets just get on with this already.'

'Seriously Cason, Uncle told me to put the blindfold on you. Once I lead you there, I'm supposed to put on a blindfold as well. Trust me.'

Trust me.

This were 2 words that Cason was not taking seriously at all now. At this point, he began feeling suspicious.

All the way from Auntie, to buying the Bob Marley shirt, to the dinner, to Uncle and his secretive tendencies. Who the hell were these people and why did they invite Cason to the family in the first place? Was there some agenda?

Cason looked around and he was clearly in the middle of nowhere. If he were to die, his family would have no clue. He did hear some horror stories of Americans traveling overseas and being robbed for everything. Was that going to happen to Cason?

'No Ivan, I'm not letting you put a damn blindfold on me. You know what, I don't know if any of this is a good idea.'

'Cason, this does not look good, I completely get your perspective. But the thing is, you just need to trust me.'

Cason wanted to yell that he didn't trust him for this shady situation but didn't want to be mean.
Once again, Cason expressed his hesitancy.
'I don't know. You have to understand how weird this seems.'

'I get it. Just calm down and take the risk.'

Once again, strategic risks came into Cason's mind. Thus far, he had done a good job of not being such a scaredy cat.

If he were to die, he would die.
But if he were not to die, then this could simply serve as the roller coaster that had been Bahamas thus far.

'Alright Ivan, do what you gotta' do.'

They both got out the car and Ivan put the blindfold on him. Then he grabbed Cason's palm and puts it on his shoulder and guided him up the hill.

All Cason could do was feel the wind on his face and the crunching of the sticks under his feet. He wasn't quite nervous anymore, he was more curious about what the hell was going to happen next.

There was some zigzagging that was taking place, and some, 'hey not that way,' from Ivan.

Eventually, Ivan began slowing down.

'Update??' Cason asked.
'We are here.'

14

Cason could hear Ivan putting the blindfold on himself as well.

'Now what? Cason asked.

'Now we wait,' Ivan said.

'For how long?'

'Uncle didn't say that.'

So, the 2 waited for what felt like an eternity. In the first 10 minutes, they were talking a little about what to expect. Still, Ivan was being pretty secretive. He wasn't going to say everything.

Cason began worrying again.
What if there were wolves and bears looking at him like lunch? He heard a bunch of chirping and movement around them. Was this Uncle guy playing some game from behind the scenes?

Eventually, they had been standing for so long that it felt like his knees were getting numb. Cason began sitting down.

'Hey Cason, are you sitting down?'

'Yea, my legs are sore. I have no clue when he's going to be here.'

'Stand up!! Quick, stand up!!'

'Why?' Cason asked as he sprang back up.

'When Uncle gives orders, he expects us to follow it Cason. We can't be breaking the rules *at all*. Just know that we are going to have to stand until Uncle comes. You aren't sitting anymore, are you?'

'No.'

Cason was standing and now he was getting irritated. They had been waiting for 1 hour in this dark area with blindfolds on. What kind of BS was this?

Especially from a family who was so picky with time. The head honcho can't even honor a time limit?

Cason could only daydream as to what was going to happen. One time, Cason saw one of his favorite singers doing a bunch of intense workouts. The video ended with:
'Everyone wants to be a singing superstar, but only a few people want to put in the work.'

That video left a strong impression on Cason.

He wondered why this singer was working out so hard for. He's just singing, not getting ready for a boxing match. But it was clear that this singer knew something that Cason didn't.

In future interviews, the singer said that in order to be a prolific singer, he had to be in shape. The voice does not just come from the mouth like a lot of newbies think. Instead, the voice comes from the entire body. When someone speaks, their entire body rings. So, it was imperative to make sure the singer took care of the ENTIRE body.

Did creative fields require some kind of physicality that outsiders were unaware of?

Was Uncle going to physically train Ivan and him in this dark forest like area?

As he was thinking about what was going to happen, he could hear footsteps.

'Hey Ivan, do you hear footsteps?'

'Yea.'

'What if it's a bear?'

'I haven't heard about too many bears in Bahamas before.'

'But what if it's a bear?? Ivan, I don't know if I like bears...'

The footsteps got closer.

'You 2 be quiet!'

It was Uncle's voice.

Cason was relieved that it was Uncle and not a bear.

'Both of you take off your blindfolds.'

They both took off their blindfolds.
It was dark, but Uncle set up a few portable lamps to create some shine.

Before they could even get adjusted and comfortable, Uncle yells out:
'Say the alphabet backwards.'

Both look at each other confused. Alphabet backwards? That would require writing it down, not reciting it out loud…

Ivan went first.
'Um, z, y, x….'

Then he got stumped.

Uncle looked over to Cason.

'Z, y, x w, v….'

Uncle looked at both of them disapprovingly. He once again said:
'Say the alphabet backwards.'

Both attempted again.
Both failed again.

Uncle repeated:
'Say the alphabet backwards. Are you listening?'

Both attempted again.
Both failed again.

At this point, Uncle was clearly getting agitated.
'You 2 are making this difficult for no reason. Once again, say the alphabet backwards. You need to follow simple instructions.

Bot attempted again
Both failed again.

This is when Uncle said:
'You guys can't follow simple orders without making it complex, can you?'

Cason had enough. He said:
'Uncle, we are trying our best, but saying the alphabet backwards is very difficult. Can you even do it??'

Uncle smiled at Cason.
'Why of course I can, watch.'

Uncle turns around so his back is facing Ivan and Cason then he begins saying:
'A, b, c, d, e....'

He finishes the entire alphabet.

That's when Ivan and Cason said:
'Ah...that's what you meant when you said to say the alphabet backwards??'
Uncle smirked.
'You see boys, this is your first lesson into creative writing. Writing and thinking are the same thing. The best writers are the best problem solvers.'

Cason never made that connection before. He knew that writers were artistic and very expressive. He never viewed them as problem solvers. Cason thought that was more for the engineering types.

'Wait Uncle, are creative people really problem solvers too?' Cason asked.

'Yes. Writing is frozen thoughts. Those who know how to think effectively know how to write effectively over time.'

Ivan had a question of his own.
'What did the alphabet thing have to do with writing? Were you teaching us about problem-solving skills?'

Uncle nodded his head. Then he followed it up with:
'It's more than that Ivan. The thing with plenty of newbie writers is that they make things unnecessarily complex. That's why their writing is messy and all over the place. This lesson with the alphabet showed that you don't need to be a rocket scientist to solve problems and think out of the box. Sometimes, the best way to become a better writer is by not being a rocket scientist. It's about being a child.'

'A child?' Cason asked.

'Yes, a child. How long do you think I made you wait out here?'

Cason thought about it.
'At least 1 hour.'

'You waited here for 1 hour and 24 minutes. See... the thing with a child is that they have trust. Trust to a fault. Trust to a fault is a coveted trait of a writer.'

Both Ivan and Cason asked:
'It is??'

'There is a creative spirit that lives in all of us. It seeks expression. Great writers are often conduits rather than the creators themselves. They only become a conduit by having unwavering faith and trust.'

Cason nodded his head but didn't agree with what Uncle was saying. There were plenty of occasions that Cason could see an adult having a childlike faith not being a good thing.

The reason Cason felt like that was because he was having a lot of faith with that producer who said he wasn't going to put him on the show. The reason that he messed up was because he put too much faith in the sweet words, and he felt that the producer would look out for him.

Cason had to shake off the bias.
He felt like he was viewing a lot of reality from that disturbing moment, and it wasn't right. It was best if he gave this thing with Uncle a real shot.

The both of them nodded.

'I may make you kids do some things that you may not feel good doing. But understand that there is a method to my madness.'

Uncle pointed the 2 over to a tree.

'Okay, I want you to knock that tree down.'

Ivan begins pushing at the tree.

He is unable to knock the tree down.

Ivan looks at Cason to see if he could do it. If Ivan can't do it, then Cason definitely can't. Ivan had way more muscles than Cason.

Cason tries and he is unable to knock the tree down.

Uncle gets angry.
'I said knock that tree down! The both of you! Knock that tree down right now!'
Both Cason and Ivan rush towards the tree trying to push it down, but they are unable too.

Uncle yells again:
'I said knock that tree down!'

Ivan musters up more energy to say:
'Uncle, we are trying but the tree is way too strong....'

Cason gets an idea.

Knock the tree down.

He looks at Uncle.
Then he moves Ivan out of the way.

Cason goes in front of the tree and turns his open palm into a closed fist.
Then he begins gently knocking the tree from the top to the bottom. As he is knocking the tree down, he is looking at Uncle and Uncle is looking back at him. They both begin smirking.

Ivan looked at the 2 as if he was disappointed with himself for missing such an obvious clue.

'Ah...that's what you meant!'

Uncle looks at Ivan.
'You feel that feeling, Ivan? The feeling of the answer having been there the entire time and now you are just becoming aware? Well, that's what writing is often like. Writing is a big game of problem solving in a nutshell. Just know that the answers are a lot simpler than it looks. Whether it's a plot twist, creating a relatable antagonist or finding the name of your main character. It's often the simplicity that has the most profound answers.'

This was going to be a beautiful training.

No clue why, but as Cason looked at Uncle, he began to have a childlike faith in the man. Even though he had never seen a writing from this man, there was a strong feeling in his mind that indicated to him that something was up.

This was going to be a wild ride that he wasn't expecting.

15

Cason didn't come home till 3 am. He had work at 7 am in the sandwich shop. By the time he came back, he was exhausted.

Now, it began making sense why that singer was in such great shape and was training like a fighter.

As they were training, Uncle had Ivan and Cason try to solve more problems. Problems that required a lot of critical thinking faculties.

Even though Cason wasn't moving around a lot, he still felt tired at the end of the meeting.

As he was in the car ride back with Ivan, he asked whether or not Ivan was tired.

Ivan said:
'Yes. Uncle said that those people who are thinking the most need to be in shape the most. The body burns faster when critical thinking is being exhausted.'

He didn't know that was a thing.
But Cason could see it.

He was **starving** after the meeting but it was too late to get something to eat. Probably would be best if he just slept in and snuck in a sandwich in the morning. No one would know.

As he was walking into the hotel, the host looked at him in a grimacing way.

Geez, Cason really did miss Brooke. He was thinking about that strategic risk. Would it be a strategic risk to pursue her even though she had a boyfriend?

Technically speaking, she was the one who also gave her number to Cason. Maybe she was in a bad relationship?

Cason had no clue what to think.
But in this meeting with Uncle, he learned that he **could** think.

Before this meeting, he didn't really ever look into problem solving.

The acts of turning around and saying the alphabet and knocking the tree down were so simple, yet had a level of nuance too. It's like the mind had to be trained into simplicity to perceive the solutions.

Earlier, when Cason was learning about writing, he thought it was just a creative act. But the way Uncle told him that writing was a masterclass on problem solving really fascinated his analytical mind.

For a living, Cason would crunch numbers. He spoke the language of math and formulas. Could he cross apply the world of math with the world of letters?

The idea was fascinating to him.

Here he was thinking so much about writing, but he didn't even write anything yet. Was he getting ahead of himself or was this a good sign?

One of the lessons from Uncle that stuck out was the childlike faith. As a kid, Cason was a daredevil for a short period. At that stage, he was the one who took risks, got in trouble, and made Billy look like the good one.

As Cason looked at the mirror, he had no clue when that changed. When did he go from being that bold child into a timid adult?

Cason thought about the human personality. If he were to get an x-ray of himself, he'd ask:
Where exactly is the personality? Is it on the brain area, the right leg, the chest? Where is the personality located?

Cason was trying to change his personality, but he didn't even know where it was!

Cason lied down and began looking at the ceiling.

Even though he didn't know where his personality was located, he had this thrilled feeling about experiencing his internal world to make sense of his emotions. This would be his opportunity to get to know himself.
He kept saying he wanted to be a different person after leaving the Bahamas. If he left today, there would already be a big difference.

Therefore, mission was accomplished to a certain extent. Still, this was only the beginning.

16

'Hey Billy, how have you been holding up with everything?'

Mom looked at Billy who was pretty quiet.

'I've been okay. I miss Cason, but am sure he is doing the right thing for his life.'

Both parents looked lovingly and went back to eating their food.

Since Cason left, Billy had missed him a lot. Cason was the younger brother who did his best to play it safe.

Growing up, Billy was the one who didn't seem to have anything on track. He was not a school guy and he wasn't too sure if he was going to make a living doing much.

Suddenly, he got a job as a carpenter's apprentice where he learned what it took to run a business.

The carpenter he worked for was a straight up dummy. If he could operate a business, then anyone could!

Only if his brother was business minded like he was. Billy always wished that he could go into business with his brother.

Billy was the visionary and the needle pusher, while Cason was the detail-oriented guy. If the 2 of them paired up, then they could make headways in the business space.

All entrepreneurial partnerships often have that dynamic. One guy is a big picture thinker while the other person is detail oriented.

Billy ran the idea by Cason a few times, but Cason was quick to shut it down.

'I hear you, Billy. But I'm not a good guy for business. You don't want me as your partner. All I'd do is annoy you.'

Only if Cason wasn't so close minded and actually gave it a chance then he'd be good.

The lifestyle Billy set up for himself was optimized to do whatever he wanted to do. Seriously, this was the one and only line on his business plan:
'Make fuck you money.'

Translation for:
'Do whatever I want to do.'

This is why Billy took a highly decentralized approach to business. If one business got shut down for overstepping the boundaries, all good. He had another bundle of businesses that would be cash flowing for him.

Billy knew how important money was. Without money, it was easy to be fearful, not fearless.

Had Billy been caught on national television while drunk, he would have been sad for driving under the influence. But he would've gotten over the rut much quicker. Even if he did go viral, he'd know that the pain would eventually end.

Ever since Billy began making money, he felt bigger and limitless. He felt the exact opposite in the come-up stages. The first 4 years of his business journey was met with a series of failures, losses, and more failures.

During those times, he battled depression and had to pull himself out of darkness by himself. As his business picked up, he learned that others simply didn't think like him.

All his buddies processed life through the lens of a worker. They'd ask questions about benefits, a steady paycheck, and a Roth IRA.

They couldn't speak Billy's language of innovation and profitability. That's why Billy struggled with tough times in the beginning. That's also why he got close to his mom in the beginning of his business journey.

His mom would often detail what it was like when she was setting up her business in the initial stages. How much of a headache it was, how much sacrifices were required and how many friends she lost.

His mom said that she would **never** exchange the process for anything. One of the first times she saw a person wearing one of her dresses at the airport, it made her feel so good.

'Entrepreneur's push the world forward, son. If you ever need to talk or a need a sounding board, I'll be here. Understand this.'

Billy understood it. That's what kept him going for the first couple of years.

Nowadays, he was making a lot of money. Money that he would reinvest back in his business to grow his empire some more.

Money was just a couple of digits on a screen. The digits were no longer a thing, they were a concept. A concept which represented:
'I can really do whatever I want.'

That's why Billy wanted Cason to take business a bit more seriously. If Cason had a few businesses that he could call his own, then he wouldn't be shitting bricks at the thought of getting fired.

Cason just didn't have the guts.

What changed?

When they were growing up, Cason was the daredevil for a while. One time, when their parents went to a wedding across town, Cason was the one who suggested they drive their parent's car.

They were only 9 at the time!

That was when Cason had this childlike wonder that made him fun to hang out with. No clue when, but Cason slowly developed into a coward and would get scared by his own shadow.

Billy wished that Cason was changing and developing while he was at the Bahamas.

Simply going to Bahamas was somewhat risky for a guy like Cason. No plan, no job, little money. That's not the type of behavior that Cason was often involved in.

Billy missed his brother.

However, he would endure missing him as long as he could get his brother to be a man with wings.

17

'Hi,' read the text message on Cason's phone.

Who the hell was 839-439-0432?
He thought about it for a second...
Who was this??

'Hey sorry, I don't have this number. Who is this?'

Send.

Cason could see typing bubbles.

'Oh my God, this is Brooke! You didn't save my number? Jerk!'

When Cason saw that it was Brooke texting him, his heart dropped. He thought about her a lot ever since she left. He wished that he took more strategic risks with her. If she was texting him, that meant he may have to capitalize on this strategic risk.

As he was about to type back, his manager comes:

'Hey Cason, get off your phone. We are packed and Ivan needs your help up front!!'

'Coming!'

Before he went to the front, he quickly texted:
'Brooke! How are you??'

Then he stuck his phone in his pocket and went back to making subs.

The next 2 hours were back to back customers. He was getting irritated.

Right after he sent the text to Brooke, he felt his phone vibrate in his pocket. Brooke must have been a fast texter.

Him keeping her waiting for so long was not a good look. What if Brooke got mad and never talked to him again??

He couldn't even leave because it was only him and Ivan making sandwiches while the manager was guarding the cash register.

Small things began making him angry. When someone would ask for extra pickles, he'd roll his eyes.

How many pickles does this fatass want?? Hurry up already!!!

2 hours turned into 2-hours and 20 minutes. That's when the store finally began getting empty.

'Hey Ivan, I need to use the bathroom.'

'What?? I need to use the bathroom too! Let me go first!'

'No Ivan, this is important. I need to go now.'

'Okay man, but hurry up!!!'

Cason rushes to the back and takes his phone out of his pocket. 'Hey, can we talk?' was the text message from Brooke.

Cason began thinking about how to respond. He wanted to play it cool but not too cool where it made him look disinterested.

At first, he wrote:
'Sure.'

No, that's too bland. Spice it up!

'Sure. What's up?'

This was better but it doesn't explain why he was so late. Spice it up even more!

'Hey Brooke sorry, got very busy at work. Sure, what's up?'

Yes, much better.
Send.

Cason was waiting on the toilet seat in suspense. Maybe she was going to take a long time to respond back because he took so long.
Luckily, that wasn't the case.
She began typing back.

'Hey Cason, just wanted to see if you wanted to hang out some time? I recall you asking me on a date and I'm single now. Would love to get to know you more.'

What???
No way!!

Was this really happening or was he dreaming?

He quickly writes:
'Sorry to hear about your past relationship. But yea, sure. How about today?'
Send.

Brooke begins typing.
'Sure. What do you want to do?'

Cason had to quickly think of something.

'How's coffee? Or am I the only one who drinks coffee that late? Lol.'
Send.

Brooke begins typing again.
'Hehe, no there are more people like you and I'm one of them.'

Cason looks up some places around the area. Then he quickly sends her the address to see if she would be down to meet up. She agreed and the time was finalized.
Wow.
Did Cason really just get a date?

He was a little embarrassed when she told him earlier that she was in a relationship. But what seemed like a loss earlier slowly became a win in the long run.

He sat on the toilet seat absorbing what just happened.

Feeling light.

That's when he hears a pounding on the door.

'Hey Cason, what the hell! You said you were going to be quick.'

18

Cason gets to the coffee place to only see Brooke already there. She seems super happy to see him and gives him a big hug.

He hugs her back.

Brooke says:
'What's up stranger! Long time no talk.'
She said the *long time no talk* in a sarcastic way because it hadn't been too long.

Cason jokingly said:
'I know, right? About time you stopped being a stranger.'

Cason used his sandwich money to buy her coffee and they both were now getting situated.

'What's up stranger? Enjoying the Bahamas so far?' Brooke asked.

He nodded his head and told her about the new job he had.
'You are looking at a sandwich artist at the moment.'

She laughed easily to his jokes. Brooke had this open personality that was easy to get along with. Very little tension and easy to create conversations.

Even though the conversation was easy, Cason wondered, *why?*

It seemed like everything was going too well. She randomly accepts his date, and the conversation was going so smoothly.

Does she need something?

Last time Cason checked, he was far from a ladies man.

As the conversation continued, there was one point there was a silence in the interaction.

Cason decided to fire of a more personal question.
'So Brooke, what happened with your relationship if you don't mind me asking?'

Brooke's smile turned sad.

She was noticeably bothered by the question but her facial expressions showed that she knew the question was coming sooner or later.

Cason topped it off with:
'But you don't have to tell me if you want to! I was just curious.'

Brooke gathered herself.
'We had been fighting a lot recently. He is someone who can get violent at times. There were a handful of times I took him back. But now, it was the final straw.'

Cason looked at her forearms and saw some bruises as if there was a large menacing hand that grabbed and pulled her.

'So, he hit you? Again, if any of the questions are too personal, no need to answer it.'

'It wasn't just the physical abuse, Cason. It was the words too. This guy is a wordsmith. He's *very* good with words and knows how to paint the picture very well. Let's just say he knew how to paint me as a loser.'

'You being a loser, Brooke? You are far from that!'

'Am I really? I mean I'm closer to my 30s than my 20s and have nothing to show for it. All I do is work desk jobs at hotels and do work that can be automated in a few years. I feel like he is somewhat right. Especially because he is pretty successful. He has a few businesses and employs a lot of people in the Bahamas.'

'Just because he employs a lot of people does not mean much, Brooke. My dad always told me that it was character that was king. If he was someone with high character, he wouldn't do stuff like that to you.'

Cason was an analytical mind though. He wondered if Brooke had any bad habits that caused this guy to react this way. Of course, he wasn't going to ask a question like that. He just sat there silently waiting for Brooke to break the silence. She was indicating with her body language that she had much more to say.

'I began dating him was I was a teenager. We are all we knew. He never cheated and I never cheated either. The thing was that he began elevating in his field out of nowhere. You won't believe how catty other women can be towards women. There were so many women who would blatantly flirt with him right in front of me.'

'Really??'

'Yea, really! At first, he was too much of a bozo to notice. But later, he was finding out that he had other options. Well, I had options too. Still, guys knew not to ever flirt with me in front of him. While the other girls weren't as respectful.'

'So, what happened?'

'When he started to get all this attention from these other women, he began to get this high and mighty attitude. This was around the same time when his business started to take off even more. It just made me feel inferior.'

'I don't know how you can ever feel inferior. You really are perfect.'

Then the 2 became silent.

Whoa, was that too much? That statement could be interpreted as creepy or borderline thirsty.

'You really mean that, Cason?'

Never mind.
He spoke too soon.
Maybe it wasn't creepy at all.

'Of course, Brooke. You are enthusiastic, pretty, and a very good conversationalist. That first day I came to the Bahamas, I was very nervous. But you made it so easy for me to get acclimated. Thank you very much.'

'Well Cason, you're very mysterious. What's up with you?'

'What do you mean?'

'I mean.... WHO ARE YOU??'

The 2 chuckled at the question.
Only if Brooke new how deep the question was.

'I am a Martian.'

She began laughing.

'I mean who are you, Cason? What interests you?'

Cason thought about it for a second.
'Um, I like writing.'

'You write??'

'No, not yet. But I will be soon. Soon, I'll be a great writer.'

Brooke's face turned confused.
'Wait... You like writing but you haven't written anything? Then how do you know you like writing?'

That's a question Cason couldn't answer.

'Um… that's a good question. I just know. I wished I could answer it better.'

'What do you like about writing?'

'Well Brooke, you know how you asked me who I am? Unfortunately, I have no clue to that answer. That's one of the reasons I came to the Bahamas in the first place. I sort of wanted to find myself and create myself.'

'I know exactly what you mean. I've been like that too, Cason. I never really got the chance to understand who I was. Especially because I had been helping my mom with her store for so long. I know exactly where you are coming from.'

She gave Cason's forearm a strong squeeze.

The squeeze made Cason feel like she was feeling sorry for him. He may have been wearing his heart on his sleeve too much. Better to maintain some mystery. He quickly bought the spotlight back on her.

'Anyways Brooke, when are you thinking about dating again? Going to enjoy being single for a while?'

'Well, I'm not the kind of girl to just hook up with someone. But yea, I am going to enjoy being single and find myself. We'll be each other's *discovering ourselves* buddies.

'Team lost!' said Cason.

She busts out laughing.

Hopefully, Cason wasn't getting friend zoned. A woman like Brooke was **exactly** his type.

19

'When are we actually going to do something, Uncle?!' Ivan yelled.

For the past hour, they had been staring at a tree.

At first, Cason was annoyed. But now he was sort of getting what Uncle was trying to teach.

As Cason kept looking at the tree, he kept noticing different things about it. Different things he didn't notice at the first glance. He wasn't too sure why Uncle was making them stare at the tree, but thus far, it was enough to make him accept the challenge.

After another hour had passed, Uncle told them to stop staring at a tree.
They got in a circle to begin a discussion.

'Okay Uncle, you had us staring at a tree for 2 hours. My back hurts and ants have been biting away at my ass. Explain yourself!' Ivan said.

'Before I explain myself kids, I want you to explain why you think I made you look at a tree for 2 hours.'

Cason's arm sprang up.

'Yes Cason?'

'Because you wanted us to notice details.'

'And?'

'And? I don't know an and. I just thought it was because you wanted us to notice details.'

'Noticing details is a byproduct of being present.'

Noticing details is a byproduct of being present.

This was probably an insight that Cason was going to have to meditate on.

'Listen boys, it doesn't matter what you look at for 1 hour, 2 hours, 3 hours and so on... Any object out there holds the answers to the universe.'

Ivan and Cason both blurt out:
'Answers to the universe??'

Uncle nods his head.

Ivan sarcastically says:
'What if I stare at racoon shit for 2 hours?'

'You'll find the answers to the universe.'

'Uncle, you are losing me,' Ivan said.

'The object doesn't matter, Ivan. What matters is the repeated act of bringing your mind back to a target. That's concentration. Concentration builds 1 pointedness. And the 1 pointedness is what unlocks a theme mind.'

Cason wasn't being as judgmental as Ivan was. Lowkey, while Cason was staring at that tree for 2 hours, he noticed he felt like he was more than his body. He felt like his mind was still and that he knew a lot. He felt like he was connected with the tree. Uncle had Cason's curiosity.

'Concentration skills will allow you to create on autopilot, Ivan and Cason. See, when some people want to be more creative, they start doing a bunch of goofy things. They start traveling all over the place, getting high, and dressing like a peacock. Nothing wrong with those, however, the answer is much simpler. The answer is to focus on **one**.'

Now Ivan was paying attention.

'Creativity turns the mind from a galaxy to a universe. Any object out there in this world, when it's fully focused on serves as the key to learning and creativity, make sense?'

Both of them nodded their heads. This was pretty interesting. Simplicity was the name of the game. Occam's Razor talked about how simplicity often had the most profound truth.

Uncle continued:

'You guys will soon be writing, but I want you guys to think correctly first.'

Body language wise, it didn't seem like Ivan was appreciating the lesson. It seemed like Uncle was too unorthodox and wasn't giving enough time to the writing part.

Uncle could sense the tension.
He talked about how Abraham Lincoln would spend extra hours sharpening the blade, so chopping the tree was light work.

Cason became curious and wanted to know more. After the meeting, he walked up to Uncle and eagerly asked for homework.

Uncle said:
'I want you to get an eraser and stare at it for at least 10 minutes a day. Whenever your mind waivers, bring your mind back to the target.'

'Okay, I can do that. Does it have to be an eraser or can it be something else?'

'It can be anything else.'

'Okay Uncle.'

20

As strange as it may seem, the one object that Cason kept staring at was a picture of Brooke. He was invited to her new hotel one day and she had a few pictures of herself with friends. Cason stole one. Of course, she wouldn't notice!

He would spend 10 minutes a day staring at that image. Cason wanted her to be his girlfriend really badly.

Even though Cason was 25 years old, he never had a girlfriend. He always found women attractive, but the idea of talking to them and keeping them interested for a long period of time seemed like a foreign concept to him.

He wanted it to work out with Brooke.

For the past couple of days, they had been hanging out more. Even though he didn't make a move on her yet, he felt like she would be open to something happening.

Cason believed in the whole strategic risk mindset, but he thought going in for a kiss and possibly being denied would be too painful.

Later today, they were going to go speedboating in the ocean of Bahamas.

He hated anything too risky. He feared driving into a rock with his speedboat. Nevertheless, since he wanted to impress her, he agreed.

Soon, he would be going to meet up with her.
Right now, he kept bringing his mind back to the photo of Brooke. Each time he bought his mind back on target, he'd feel more confident.

Something about bringing the distracted mind back to a target was felt in the heart. This Uncle guy must know what he's talking about. A lot of the principles that he was teaching was not taught in other places.

He continued to stare at the picture.
He stared for another 10 minutes at the picture then got ready.

1 hour passes by.

Now he is walking on the beach.
Clearly, there were a lot of tourists around the area. Cason must have had a local look because many people came to him asking for directions. When he said that he was visiting too, they looked at him suspiciously like he was an employee who was tired of interacting with the tourists.

He followed the tourists to the beach. From the corner of his left eye, he could see a woman, wearing a black and red bikini sitting on the sand.

It was Brooke.

He walked towards her.

The sand was white.
The weather was beautiful.

She was staring off into the ocean. When Cason came and said hi, she got startled.

'Hey Cason! What's up?? Are you ready to do some speed boating?'

'Not really. I keep getting scared that I'm going to hit a rock and die.'

He was surprised that he blurted that out so quickly. Especially because he wanted to look brave in front of her.

Rather than judging him, she gave a delicate laugh and said: 'You have nothing too worry about. I'm going to be the one driving.

'What?? No way! I'm going to be driving.'

'Nope, I already called it.'

They both giggled and went to the men who were renting out the speedboats by the shore.

The men showed the 2 how to ride the speedboat, the maximum distance they could go, and then gave some final words before they went onto the sea:
'You guys make such a cute couple!!'

Cason didn't say anything.

Brooke didn't say anything either as if indicating she took the comment as a compliment.

For the next 30 minutes, Cason sat on the back seat while Brooke scurried along the ocean. They went by islands and could see the fishes through the crystal-clear water.

It was a blast.

After the speedboating, they went to a different part of the island to do snorkeling.

At this point, it was getting very windy. So, the snorkeling experience was not too pleasant.

Any time Cason would go down with the mouth breathing tube, he'd get water pouring into the tube which he would accidentally swallow.

Also, fighting the waves was painful, and his muscles began cramping. But he didn't make any excuses. He just wanted to make sure that Brooke was having a good time.

After a couple of hours, they had seen all the fishes they could have possibly seen and then went back to the beach.

Brooke laid down a towel for both of them on the beach. No umbrellas needed because the sun was covered by the clouds.

Cason lied down.
Brooke lied down.

They talked for a while.

She asked more about his life in the US.
He asked more about her childhood and they continued to bond.

Suddenly, Cason's heart was firing through the roof. He really wanted to kiss her.

He made the decision to go for it.

This was going to be a strategic risk. Thus far, she was the one who pretty much asked him on a date, she was the one who texted him first and she was the one who kept asking him questions.

For sure, this was the perfect time.

As they were talking....
Cason grabbed her by the neck and went close towards her for a kiss.

Soon as he was close, she turned her face so he landed on the cheek.

Embarrassed, he quickly sprang backwards to his side of the blanket.

Brooke could sense the embarrassment and said:
'Sorry Cason. I really like you, but I don't want to move too fast with you. Is that okay?'

Cason nodded his head without saying a word but he was pretty embarrassed and angry. It felt like she was leading him on.

hat did she mean that they were moving too fast?

They had hung out a few times by now and everything had been going so well.

'You sure it's okay, Cason?'

'Yep.'

Cason was visibly irritated at this point and he got up.

'I think it's time we begin heading out....'

Brooke looked surprised especially because it seemed like they were in the middle of a great conversation.

'You sure everything is okay? I'm sorry, I just don't want to rush anything, okay? I would definitely be open to seeing you some more.'

Cason didn't know if he wanted to do that.

Is this what strategic risks were going to be like?

Sure, it could open up a lot of opportunities. But when he striked out, the pain would really sting.

The pain of being shut down for a kiss from a girl that he had pretty much been meditating on was hurtful.

21

The next day at work felt strange. Judging by the body language, Ivan could tell something was wrong with Cason.

'You okay, bud?'

'Yes, I'm okay.'

'You sure?'

'Actually Ivan... No, I'm not. Have you ever been in love before?'

Ivan nodded his head.

'What happened to her?'

Ivan got visibly sad...
'Well, I was going to marry her. But her dad was an army guy. She was moving around a lot. She ended up moving away bro. Why do you ask?'

'Did you ever think about making the whole long-distance thing work?'

'We tried. But when she moved to Italy, she found a new guy and ended it with me. I still love her to this day. That's why I haven't been too open to dating. What about you? Why do you ask?'

Cason went onto tell Ivan that he never had a girlfriend before and that he wanted to make Brooke his girlfriend. He talked about the recent rejection.

Ivan began laughing.

'Haha, sorry man, I don't mean to laugh. It's just the whole thing with girls, they're so emotional. What are we going to do with them, right?'

Cason did notice the difference in dynamic between men and women. Why the big difference? Why was a lot of art often based around heartbreaks?

This feeling that Cason was feeling of being rejected didn't feel good at all. It's almost like when his drunk driving went public.

'Hey Ivan, we are pretty free for the rest of the day. You mind taking care of the shop? I need to do some thinking really quick.'

'Yea Cason, sure.'

Cason wasn't going to do much thinking. Instead, he had some questions for Uncle.

22

'You know a heartbreak is one of the best times to become a creative writer, Cason.'
Uncle told him.

Uncle had a cigar in his mouth.

'There was one time I found out my dad and I were both going to be working in the same company. It was strange because I was able to rise up fast in the company while my dad struggled. He was a lot older and didn't have the drive he once had.'

Uncle was talking while puffing on the cigar.

'It was heartbreaking to see how my dad was not the powerful man that he once was. He seemed a lot softer and childlike. I wrote that into a story. Walk with me, Cason.'

Cason walked with him.
Then Uncle walked Cason into the basement.

Cason had never seen the basement before. He was expecting it to be dirty, but it was not dirty. Instead, it was polished. More polished than any other room in the house.

Cason saw a huge library of books. This was one of the finest bookcases he had ever seen.

'Wow!!! There are so many books there. Did you read all of that?'

Uncle smiled.
'I read half of that and I wrote the other half of that.'

'What??'

'That's correct. Which one do you want to see first?'

Cason quickly said he wanted to see the books that Uncle had written. Apparently, he was this famous writer, but Cason hadn't seen a shred of his writing yet.

Uncle walked him towards the left side of the book case where there must have been at least 100 books.

'You want to see the fiction or the nonfiction?'

'You write both?'

Uncle nodded.

'Fiction.'

Uncle grabbed one of the fiction books and gave it to Cason.

Cason looked at the book. Beautiful glossy cover design with 'Wally' on the front. On the bottom, it wrote 'Uncle.'

'Wait a minute! Is your real name, Uncle?'

'No, it's a pen name.'

'Then what's your real name?'

'It doesn't matter. At this point, I go by Uncle.'

'What's the story with that??'

Uncle was motioning to Cason to have a seat with him on the sofas.

Cason grabbed the book and looked through it. He skimmed a few pages and read some of the dialogue. The book must have been at least 400 pages. There were so many books like this!! This man was prolific, no denying that.

Uncle sat Cason down. Then he said:

'My real name is Robert Watch but I went by Uncle as a pen name. The reason why was because when I was a little kid, I'd play a game with my brother and his friends where I'd role play as Uncle Robert.'

'Okay...'

'By the time my writing career began, I initially went by my name. I wrote a lot of nonfiction books on self-improvement, mindset, and habit building. But there came one day when I was watching the movie, the Mask. You ever seen that? It's the movie with Jim Carrey.'

'I've seen that movie a lot. I think I lost count of how many times I've watched it!'

'You know when Jim Carrey would wear the mask, he would become someone brand new?'

Cason nodded his head.

'Well, I wanted that feeling. I felt like with nonfiction, I was writing too much about who I already was and what I knew. But I wasn't taking any risks. Do you know that feeling of not taking risks even when you want to?'

Cason aggressively nodded his head like:
Don't even get me started!

'Well, one day, I was writing by myself and I kept hitting writer's block. I'll share in a future lesson why writer's block is a myth. But my younger self didn't know that. I kept hitting this wall. So, I decided to do something."

'What did you do?'

'I decided to change my name. I went back to the past. I became known as Uncle.'

'Um…why?'

'Because what is the name really? It's just a couple of scribbles that we identify with. If someone gets our name wrong, we *feel* it. When we *feel* it, it shows what it means to us. I felt like when I changed my name, I didn't have to be the same self that Robert was. I could be **different**. It was a linguistic version of me putting the mask on like Jim Carrey.'

Cason never thought of this concept before. It was sort of like Uncle was his alter ego. The alter ego allowed him to take more risks.

'What causes embarrassment, Cason?'

'I'm not too sure...'

'Think about it. When was the last time you were very embarrassed?'

2 moments quickly sprang into Cason's mind. One was of him being denied for a kiss and the other was of him showing up on DUI Dummies.

What did those 2 moments have in common?

'Okay Uncle, I have a few of those moments pulled up. Now what?'

'Well, the reason that you became embarrassed was because you assigned a lot of importance to those moments. If someone called you an alien, you wouldn't care. But if someone did something to you that affected your reality, then you would feel embarrassed.'

Cason agreed but he still couldn't tell what the point was.

Uncle continued.
'So, when I changed my name, I quit moving so fearful. At first, I was more so writing for my audience. Nowadays, I write for my younger self.'

'Your younger self?'

'Yes. I write for that younger Robert who was playing Uncle. That's my target audience. By having that target audience, it becomes way easier to write freely. Uncle served as a reminder of who I was writing to.'

'Okay, I get why you go by Uncle when you write. But why go by Uncle in your personal life?'

'Nowadays, my reality is blurred. My life's work **is** me. You see all those books right there?'

He pointed at the book shelf.

Cason nodded.

'Those books have defined who I am.'

'I get it, Uncle.'

Initially, Cason came to see what he should do about the heartbreak he had recently. He still didn't have an answer to that. Should he think of a cool name as well?

'Uncle, you think I should think of a cool name as well or something?'
'You eventually will have to. I'm glad you came today to seek advice but be patient. I am working you and Ivan up the fundamentals. Your time will eventually come.'

'Great.'

'Now go home and great some rest.
You are going to need it for tonight.'

23

Cason completely forgot about the meeting that Ivan and him were going to have with Uncle at night. If he remembered that, then he would have just taken a nap after leaving work early.

He was yawning away in Ivan's car.

'Hey man, I'm the one who let you leave early and you are the one yawning??'

They both laughed.
They continued to drive on the dark roads into the forest.

They arrived.

Uncle said:
'Both of you, get on your knees.'

Strange request, but they both did it.
Uncle dropped a paper and pencil in front of both of them.

'Okay, now I need you to write about your fears.'

Finally! Some writing.

The paper had a lot of lines on it. Guess they would be given a lot of time to write.

'You guys have 10 minutes to fill up the entire page.'

Ivan and Cason both became alarmed.

'10 minutes?? This will require at least 40 minutes Uncle,' Ivan said.

'No, it will require only 10 minutes. Or else.'

'Or...or...else?' Cason asked stammering.

'Yes, or else.'

Uncle pulled out a pistol from his pocket.

'Finish your writing in 10 minutes or else I will have to shoot your foot.'

'What?? That's a joke!' Ivan said.

Without second notice, Uncle fired off a bullet right by Ivan's foot.

Both Ivan and Cason could feel the breeze from the high-speed bullet.

'Uncle, what the fuck?? You almost fucking shot me!!' Ivan roared.

'10 minutes. I don't care about grammar or anything like that. Just fill up the pages. Since you fought me on this and didn't put faith in me, you have 8 minutes. Begin.'

Cason was terrified. He knew that this guy had some strange tendencies, but actually firing off a gun?

The 2 began writing like their life depended on it. Their heartbeats were pounding through the roof while both their pencils were shaking.

However, they were making their way through a significant amount of the page.

'4 minutes,' Uncle said.

The 2 continued to write away.

'2 minutes.'

They were getting close to the end of the paper. Cason glanced over to Ivan's page and saw a similar amount of the page covered.

'10 seconds.'

Thank goodness!
Cason just got done.

'Time!!'

Cason and Ivan both finished the assignment.

'Okay boys, you guys fold the paper and put it in your pocket. I will tell you what you will do with that shortly.'

Ivan still looked terrified from almost getting shot …

'Uncle, were you really going to shoot me?'

'Do you want to learn writing or not?'

Ivan nodded his head.

Uncle asked again:
'Do you want to learn writing or not??'

Ivan once again nodded his head.

Cason saw the visible head nodding from Ivan but deep inside, he didn't believe Ivan.

Although Ivan used a lot of the right words in their late-night conversations, Cason began questioning the intentions of Ivan. It felt like Ivan wanted to learn writing so he could become a celebrity. It wasn't because he really appreciated the craft of writing and its transformative powers.

Was Cason being too judgmental? Because what was Cason exactly doing? He was learning writing so he could build self-confidence.

Maybe Ivan had the same intention but it was being expressed in a different way. Maybe he was trying to become a better celebrity so he could build self-confidence. Cason wasn't too sure.

'Ivan, how bad do you really want this?' Uncle asked.

'I want this really bad.'

'Good.'

He had both Cason and Ivan cross their legs and sit down. It was lecture time.

'Writer's block is a myth. This myth is typically encountered in moments of comfort.'

'What do you mean writer's block is a myth? Then why do so many people talk about suffering from it?' Cason asked.

'The reason that they suffer from this illusion is for a few reasons. They are either too focused on the end goal or they are too comfortable.'

Uncle gave them some time to take notes.

'Reason #1, the *end goal*. The best writing happens in the present moment. This is when time seizes to exist. All these modern-day self-improvement books call it the *flow state*. I like to just call it the *present*. In the present, creativity is abundant and there is no such thing as writer's block.'

They both wrote that down.

Then Uncle said:

'Reason #2 is because they are too comfortable. When you are too comfortable, you focus on the wrong things. Rather than focusing on the ideas, you become too focused on the words.'

'But aren't words a part of the ideas?' Ivan asked.

'The words are simply a way to express the idea. What happens when we are too comfortable is that the writer focuses on using the right words and completely loses focus of the bigger picture. They are too comfortable. They don't write with urgency.'

'Hm... I sort of get what you're trying to say Uncle, but I don't fully get it,' Cason said.

'When someone is too focused on the little details, they encounter the illusion of writer's block. When I pointed the pistol at you guys, you had urgency. When you have urgency, you have speed. With speed, the tendency to overthink melts away. Write this down... adrenaline plus added time equals anxiety. Adrenaline minus time equals creativity.'

Cason neatly wrote the formula down:

- Adrenaline + Time = Anxiety
- Adrenaline − Time = Creativity

'Okay Uncle, how do I exactly create adrenaline without....um ...a gun pointing at me?' asked Ivan.

Uncle reached in his pocket and pulled out 2 tiny analog timers with the spinning dial.

'You use timers.'

This was the best meeting yet. Thus far, they were both given a great opportunity to write something down. It felt like they were going through all these loopholes but now they had something to show for it.

'Anyways, here's your assignment for the next meeting. You know the writing you wrote today? I want you to edit and polish it up. You have the content, now it's just a game of fixing up the spelling, punctuation, and all of that. Make sense?'

'Yes, it makes sense,' said the students.

24

Cason was thinking if he should exchange his hotel for an apartment. He had no clue how much longer he was going to be in the Bahamas, but he didn't feel like he had answers to the questions that he was seeking.

After getting back late at night, Cason was exhausted. He was planning on doing Uncle's assignment in the morning. However, he was very curious about what it had in store.

Despite feeling tired, he pulled out the paper from his pocket.

It had a bunch of gibberish on it. A lot of words, but not too much meaning. What could possibly be so great about this...?

But as he was going through the gibberish, he could extract some meaningful information. This wasn't pure gibberish. Despite him writing all sloppy, he still had words that were comprehensible.

As he was going through the writing, he thought:
This Uncle guy may be onto something. I thought this was not going to make sense at all. But it actually makes a lot of sense.

He continued to read through the gibberish and then curiosity got the best of him. He was going to turn the writing into a final document.

When he looked at the first couple of lines, he saw:

'Withei'm tererinefe riwght now,a d a guyn is pointed towards bme. But you now whats even fmore ftireyfineting? Seeing your face palstered raroucss the faceteantionval teveloeision for your parent sna gbotehr sto see.'

This was what the writing looked like. With a a few fixes, Cason transformed the gibberish into:

'Well, I'm terrified right now, and a gun is pointed towards me. But you now what's even more terrifying? Seeing your face plastered across national television for your parents and brother to see.'

Wow! he thought.

Writing something like this was not something he could normally see himself writing. Actually, now that he was going through the entire writing, he was noticing that the entire tone he wrote with felt so different. It felt like an identity.

It felt like the identity that he was yearning for.

So, this is what writing is about. I never did this writing style where I didn't plan. I have been writing my entire life planning out everything that I was going to say, Cason thought.

He continued to clean up the passages of the writing. As he went through it, he had a beautiful draft starting at him.

He couldn't believe it. There were plenty of ideas he wrote that he couldn't believe came out of him. He was really surprising himself.

Was this the cheatcode?
Create like there is a gun being pointed at you?

He didn't know if this was the cheatcode, but he was more sold on Uncle than he was sold before.

So, he was going apply another tip...he was going to create an alternate name just like Uncle had.

What could be as catchy as Uncle?

Actually, who was he kidding?? Uncle was lame! Cason could do better than that.

Hm... What about Curious Cason?

Nah, that sounds too much like Curious George, the monkey. What about Captivating Cason?

No, that sounds like he was about to join the Powerpuff Girls.

He had to think about it...

25

If Cason was heartbroken after the rejected kiss, he was about to be even more heartbroken.

Brooke invited him for coffee at the same place they initially met for their first date. This time, it was her suggestion. This time, she didn't seem as enthusiastic about the meetup.

He felt guilty for giving her the silent treatment for rejecting the kiss. But he would probably have another opportunity to kiss her now that he was being invited to another date.

That wasn't going to be the case.

Instead, Brooke was going to be breaking some sad news.

The sad news was that she was going to be getting back with her boyfriend.

'What?? You sure?? Didn't you say that he hit you and put you down a lot?'

'Yea Cason, he did.'

'So? Then why are you getting back with him??'

'It's because I still love him.'

Cason was processing what she had just said. How could you possibly love someone who abused you? Was this girl crazy??

He was becoming pretty upset because he answered his own question. Because now that Cason thought about it…

He loved her for the same exact reason that she loved her boyfriend. He loved her despite her flaws. That's how she must have been perceiving her boyfriend.

'You sure, Brooke?'

'Yes Cason, I'm sure. I'm so sorry if you think I led you on. I really think you are a great guy and I think you will make a girl a very happy girl one day. Just for the time being, I don't want to bring baggage to you.'

'You won't bring baggage. I'll love you through the ups and down. I'm consistent, something this guy can never be. Please give me a chance.'

Cason was surprised that he was talking like this. Normally, he wasn't an emotional guy. He was reserved and aloof.
The idea of Brooke being so close then being dragged so far was not something he was happy with.

'I'm sorry Cason, but I'm sure of this decision. I still want to keep in touch as a friend, okay?'

Now Cason's sadness turned into apathy. A friend?

No, he had enough friends. This wasn't going to be a working relationship.

'Brooke, I see what you are saying. But you know what? I think you and I just need to go our own ways. Hopefully, one day, we can run into each other again.'

'Cason, please. Can we please stay friends?'

'No Brooke, I'm sorry but let's just do our own thing.'

He got up and began walking away.

As he began walking away, he could feel tears falling down his face. This was the first time he was in love.

He was in love with a girl he had never kissed.

26

Cason pulled up his laptop and began writing away.

Uncle had him writing by hand, but now Cason was typing. Something about typing allowed him to feel uninhibited. He was a faster typer than a hand writer.

He felt intense emotions.
He could feel Brooke going to the beaches of Bahamas with her ugly boyfriend. Even though the guy was not ugly, in Cason's imagination, he was.

That's when he had an idea....

For the past couple of weeks, he began reading that one book of Uncle's. The fiction one called Wally. Wally was a breathtaking book.

It was about an autistic boy who was gifted in Chinese Checkers. The boy had a photographic memory and was going to overcome his deficiencies by being great at Chinese Checkers. There was going to be a competition that Wally went to in order to prove his Chinese Checkers mastery.
Initially, this game was just a game.

Overtime, the game of Chinese Checkers was one of the few things that was bonding US, Russia, and China. The countries were on the brink of war at any moment. However, the Chinese Checkers game was a phenomenon that all of them were interested in.

The story of Wally starts off with a kid learning to play Chinese Checkers. Overtime, it blossoms into a story about a boy with gifts who has the power of stopping a war.

The story was breathtaking. Nowadays, when Uncle spoke, people shut their mouths. It's because he was an extraordinary writer. He was someone who was capable of sharing truths in fiction. The type of truths that raw nonfiction would not be able to properly convey.

What fascinated Cason even more about the story of Wally was the Chinese Checkers part. Not how Wally was great at the game…

Instead, how great Uncle was at the game.

There were a few times Cason talked to Ivan who said that before becoming a writer, Uncle was the Chinese Checkers champion in local tournaments.

What does this really mean?

Was Wally a complete fabricated character born out of Uncle's imagination?
Or was Wally created from bits and pieces of Uncle himself?
Cason hypothesized that it was the latter.

The intense emotions that Cason was feeling were bubbling up. It was not just the Brooke incident that had him feeling like this. It was a culmination of things that had him feeling like a mess.

The past couple of months had been a roller coaster and a nightmare.

- He was a lost person without any form of personality.
- He gets caught on national TV crying like a bitch.
- He randomly leaves his family to move to the Bahamas.
- The girl he quickly fell in love with turned him down for her abusive boyfriend.

When was the nightmare going to end?
He needed a way to express himself.

You know what? I'm going to do what Uncle did, Cason thought.

Cason had been writing in his Word Document for the past couple of hours. He had dozens of pages of gibberish staring at him.

That's when he deleted everything.

He then wrote:
'The Tales of Augusto...'

By Anonymous....

27

Ivan and Cason's relationship had gotten stronger. The 2 felt like brothers at this point. There was this bond they felt ever since working with Uncle. It's like they knew something that others didn't know.

They would talk a lot about a whole bunch of topics ranging from their goals, their past, and how they were going to deal with Uncle's shenanigans.

A few of Cason's buddies were in fraternities in college. They would often talk about the fraternity experience. They talked about how it was brutal.

The process consisted of them having to memorize a bunch of facts about the fraternity, doing physical work, and pretty much being a servant to the brothers.

When Cason asked them why they put up with such pain, they would often say:
'Because I wanted to appreciate the brotherhood once I became a member.'

Cason didn't get it at the time.

Nowadays, he was starting to get it.

People put value in what they work for. There was this famous quote by Thomas Paine which went like:

'The harder the conflict the more glorious the triumph. What we obtain too cheap, we esteem too lightly. It is dearness only that gives everything its value. I love the man that can smile in trouble, that can gather strength from distress and grow.'

Had Uncle made this process easy, Cason wouldn't have known if this process would have been congruent for him in the first place. But the late-night meetings, having a gun pointed at them, staring aimlessly at a tree allowed him to appreciate the craft of writing.

Ivan and Cason would often talk about writing in 2 completely different languages.

Cason talked about the craft in general. How words were perception programmers, how to build a plot, and create a dialogue.

Cason would ask Ivan if he had a certain method of editing once he was done creating the content.
However, the talk of the writing craft didn't interest Ivan much. He was more so interested in how much money writing was going to make him.

Cason would be lying if he didn't think about the money as well, but that was not his main focus. His main focus was the art. From the art, whatever money came, came. The money was seen as the orange juice, not the orange.

Even when Cason bought up the variety of fiction books that Uncle wrote, Ivan didn't seem to care. He just said 'nice' and then changed topics.

Ivan probably knew something Cason didn't. Maybe Cason was being a tad bit naive. The last thing Cason wanted to be was a starving artist. He wanted his words to turn into a business.

The conversation with Ivan turned very dark.

'Cason, I think a big reason I want to make it is because I want to get my mom and sisters out of that crammed house. It upsets me she has to work so hard. After a long day's work, she sleeps on the floor. I love Uncle and Auntie for taking us in without second thought after my dad's passing but I just want a better life for my mom and sisters, you know?'

Cason wanted to ask how his father passed away, but he did know if he should. That's when **strategic risks** popped in his mind.

'You don't mind if I ask what happened to your dad, do you Ivan?'

Ivan was silent...

Cason quickly realized that he overstepped the boundaries.

'Actually, never mind. Do you read by the way?'

'Cason, I will tell you. Just give me a second.'

Ivan gathered himself. Clearly, he was entering a conversation topic that made him uncomfortable.

After taking a few seconds to compose himself, he said: 'My dad was killed by a drunk driver.'

Cason's heart dropped.

Ivan continued.

'My dad was coming out of a long day's work. He was an honest man who was a brick layer. I really learned a lot about work ethic when he was alive, he worked hard so we wouldn't have to work so hard. He was a religious man who prayed to God. He was active in the community and always gave back. I can't really think of anything that was wrong with my dad.'

'How was your relationship with him?'

'My relationship with him was great. He taught me what it was like to be a man, not a boy. My dad would always say that a boy worked for himself while a man worked for others. Whenever I'd be acting selfish and not sharing with my sisters, he would ask these strategic questions to make me give back to them. He wouldn't ever tell me to do something, he'd just guide with questions. You know what I mean?'

'Mhm...'

'He was a good guy. Rarely argued with my mom or yelled at me and my sisters growing up...'

Then Ivan took a pause.
He had to gather himself again.

'One night, he was coming back from a long day. And ...and... Some idiot was driving on the wrong side of the road. He crashed head on to my dad's car. Both of them died on the spot.'

Ivan began crying.

Cason put his hand on Ivan's back and began tapping him as if saying, 'it's okay.'

'I saw the picture of the fucker who killed my dad. It was a middle-aged guy who was apparently sad because his wife was going to leave him. He had been drinking too much and decided to get behind the wheel. Why do people drink alcohol and get behind the wheel? That's something that I will never get. Anyone who does that is a coward. Fuck drunk driving!!'

The memories of his father began flooding Ivan's mind. He was reliving the horrors of the police officers coming in and knocking on his door late at night with the news.
'I'm sorry, but your father was killed tonight, young man.'

Cason's heart was beating fast.
Ironically, this would have been the perfect time to share why Cason was **really** in the Bahamas. How he had gone viral for drunk driving. If there was anything known ask strategic risks, this was it.

Tell Ivan why you are really here. He will be angry at you, but will forgive you over time. Just do it. It's not right to hold this secret. Especially since you 2 have been bonding as of late.

Cason was freezing up. Seeing Ivan crying and getting furious at the drunk driver was enough to make Cason sweep his secret under the rug.

He went back to consoling Ivan.

'Cason, that's why I want to be successful. Some of the richest people in the world know how to write. I want to be like that too. I know you and I are going to the top, I just know it. We need to push each other to be great, no matter how much we are struggling. Does that make sense?'

'It makes all the sense in the world, Ivan.'

28

Uncle had a different meeting setup tonight.
Or better yet, today.

This was the first meeting that was going to be in the daytime.

Once Ivan and Cason got to the location, Uncle had a few supplies set up. He had chairs, a desk, and a pile of books.

'Kids, today you will be reading."

'And?' asked Ivan.

'That will be it.'

For the next 2 hours, they all read at the meeting location.

As 2 hours were wrapping up, Uncle had them put their books down. Pop quiz time.

'So kids, do you know why we read today?'

Both shook their heads.

'It's because to be a great writer, you need to read a lot. Just like a body builder has to take their nutrition seriously, a writer has to take their reading seriously.'

What was the big deal about reading books specifically? Why not read blogs or newspapers? So, they asked Uncle.

'You can read whatever. Newspapers, book covers, blogs, etc. That's all optional. But what you MUST do is read books too.'

Then Ivan said:
'Why books? I mean books are so long and time consuming. I'm sure I can get the same information from of a blog. Uncle, nowadays, they have those sites that will summarize a book for you! Isn't that cool??'

'No Ivan, that's not cool. Skimping on your reading will make your writing choppy and not fluid. Here's the thing kids…reading gives you superpowers.'

That final sentence really resonated with Cason. He immediately wrote that down.

Reading gives you superpowers.

Uncle continued.
'Remember earlier how I told you that those who can concentrate at will can be creative at will?'

Both of them nodded their heads.

'Well, reading is one of the best ways to build concentration skills. Our minds have this trait called the monkey mind. This is when we are hopping from thought to thought. Like a monkey that got stung by a stingray and is hopping all over the place.'

The 2 laughed.

'The signal is the meaningful information and the noise is the chatter and junk. Those with the monkey mind have a higher noise than signal. Those who tame the monkey have a higher signal and little noise.'

Uncle bought a whiteboard today and was writing a lot of these lessons on the the board. He wrote:

Signal < Noise = Bad Writer
Signal > Noise = Good Writer

Books increase signal.

As he was writing these formulas down, he began saying:
'You see kids? Writing isn't only an art, but more importantly, a science. If you have a few formulas locked away in your mind, you will be a great writer in due time. Got it?'

Both nodded their heads.
Uncle continued praising books.

'Reading allows you to think in words. When you think in words, it becomes much easier to write in words.'

'What type of books should we read Uncle? Books on writing skills?'

'No! You read **everything**. Just like an investor reads books outside of investing alone, great writers read books outside of writing alone. Read everything.'

'Even bad books?'

'Especially bad books.'

'Why especially bad books?'

'Because bad books teach you what not do. It's like a business owner who studies the bad reviews so they could improve. If they only read the good reviews, then they wouldn't be aware of the pockets of opportunities to improve. When you read good and junk, what happens is that it gives you a **feel** for writing.'

This made sense to both Ivan and Cason. Especially because they were aiming to be creators not only consumers.

'How long should we read?'

'Start light and work your way up. You guys are mastering the mental sports now. Treat mental sports very similar to physical sports. A skinny guy doesn't go to the gym and immediately start benching 250 pounds. Instead, they start off light with the bar. They work on fixing their form. When they are capable of doing that, that's when they add in some weight. From there, they add on even more weight. Likewise, start reading a book for 10 minutes a day or 10 pages a day. Then gradually keep adding onto that. From there, you'll see it hard not to read. Reading will become a part of your routine like eating.'

Ivan was looking pretty disinterested at this point. This reading lecture seemed like another roadblock to actually writing. But for Cason, his eyes were lighting up.

He thought:
I can become a better writer by reading?? If so, then sign me up!!

'Okay kids, so the biggest lesson is that you can read anything and become a better writer. Make sure you are focusing while you're reading. Follow your curiosities and go where you go. Work light and build your way up. Cool?'

'Cool!!'

'Okay, meeting is done!'

29

Secretly after work and the meetings with Uncle and Ivan, Cason began publishing short stories.

There was a popular website where short story writers were able to publish their stories and have people read it.

Most of the authors showed their face. But Cason decided to remain anonymous.

The *Tales of Augusto* was the name of his short story series.

These writings were mainly a form of therapy for Cason. Cason had been reading a lot more lately.

There was one article he read about the importance of transformative arts.

He found out there where sectors all around the world where professionals used art to help their clients make sense of traumatic experiences.

There were arts of people who drew.
Arts of people who made music.

And arts of people who did poetry.

As Cason had been reading more, he had been getting more curious about the definitions of words. He always felt like he knew certain words, but the more he thought about it...he didn't really know the meanings.

Instead, he just knew it at a surface level.
One of the examples was the word, 'art.'

He used to think art meant to draw and just left it at that.

Recently, he learned that art meant to *communicate an idea*. When he learned that definition, it's like his perception shifted.

For the first time, Cason thought:
Wow! I may actually be an artist.

He took it one level further. He saw another nuance of art.
It was called language arts.

The ability to communicate ideas through words.

Although this didn't seem like a big thing to others, it was a very big deal for Cason. The reason why was because he had direction.

That's what he was looking for in the past couple of months to years. He just needed direction. Now he knew he had direction when he felt like this language arts thing was congruent to him.

This was a feeling he **never** got from accounting. With accounting, everything was a head level activity. He did accounting because he felt like he had to do it.

With language arts, it was different. He wanted to learn more about it because he thought it would be fun to learn.

More importantly, as he was writing the Tales of Augusto, the information would make sense.

Had Cason been reading random blogs on language arts without writing anything of his own, he doubted he would have gravitated towards the subject as much as he did.

With the Tales of Augusto, he aimed to make each short story better than the prior one. Each short story taught him what to do and what not to do.

Something about reading a book was different than reading a blog.

With a blog, he got the information.
However, with reading a book, he got the information and transformation as well.

After reading for a certain part of the day, he felt like he thought clearly and spoke clearly as well. The ability to think clearly meant he could write clearly as well.

The craft of writing was not just about writing well, it was also about editing.

Where he did the writing fast like a gun was being pointed towards his head, his editing style was different. His main goal with editing was to turn his writing into something pleasant.

The first time he went through the rough draft, he went through it quickly to fix the red lines showing misspelling and obvious punctuation errors.

Then he would go through it again. This time, he would mentally read his writing.

As Cason kept stacking up reps, he learned that the best writing was the writing where the mind just glided through the words.

Growing up, he hated writing because teachers would preach the exact opposite. His teacher, Ms. Charnok, would ask for all this flowery language that did nothing to move the plot forward.

When Cason began reading Uncle's writing, everything was so crisp and clear. It's like Uncle was talking right to him.

That was Cason's favorite type of writing. Where it felt like the author and him were having this 1 on 1 conversation that the rest of the world was not invited to.

That's how Cason wanted to write too.

He learned what it was like to over edit a draft. Where he was too formal.

What made Uncle's writing different was that he would occasionally use slang and colloquial language. Informality at its finest.

Why?

Shouldn't a trained writer write in a way where everything is formal?

No!

In the real world, someone doesn't say stuff like:
'May I go to the restroom?'

They often just say:
'I'm going to the bathroom.'

Some even say:
'Time to take a shit!'

It's a subtle change, but a change nevertheless. These changes were what it was like to understand the nuances of writing. Noticing little stuff like this made Cason excited.

Before when he read a book, he'd just read it. Nowadays, he'd hold the book and feel it.

He'd feel the cover.
Matte or gloss?
He'd look at the pages.
White or yellow?

Then he'd estimate how long a book would take him to read. He began viewing books like a basketball player viewed the ball.

A basketball player could clearly tell if a ball was worn out, lacking in air or was too bouncy.

One of the most stunning realizations he had was:
People do judge a book by its cover.

This may not have been fair but it was true. Cason made this insight because he was someone who judged a book by its cover!

When he initially saw a lot of books, the covers looked worn out and flat-out ugly. There was no beauty to the covers at all.

What made Uncle's books different was that it had a beautiful design. The design in the front communicated the story inside.

Art meant to communicate ideas.
One way to communicate an idea was through a picture.

It was clear that Uncle didn't just slap something on the cover, it was well thought out. He created a cover that matched the narrative in the book.

Where other authors just wrote their title and wanted the content to speak for itself, Uncle wanted the content to speak and the cover to complement!

This was something that the Apple products often did. The packaging was so beautiful on the Apple product. The product could have sucked, but that initial unpackaging experience was an **experience.**

When Cason grabbed a book from Uncle's library, there was a nice feeling in knowing that the book was in great quality and looked nice.

It's like a book had the physical parts...
which were the cover, words & pages.

But the book had a spiritual part too. The spiritual part was something that Cason was becoming more well accustomed too since he began writing the Tales of Augusto.

Ah, Augusto.
Who is Augusto?

Augusto is who Cason was and who Cason aspired to be.

The story of Augusto is about a boy who lacked identity.

Augusto decides to go on a journey. His goal is to go to every country on the planet and extract 1 lesson from each country.

Each lesson he extracts is Augusto's journey in creating himself, no longer trying to find himself.

The short stories discuss Augusto's journey around the world.

It was a dream of Cason's to one day travel to every country. He needed perspective of those countries to bring Augusto to life.

He also felt like him and Augusto had this synergistic relationship with one another. Augusto only had life because of Cason. In order to give Augusto more life, Cason **needed** to grow.

He needed to travel.
Experiment.
And take strategic risks.

From there, he'd be able to inject more life into Augusto!

What a lovely dance.
Cason breathes life into Augusto.
And Augusto breathes life back into Cason.

The first day Cason saw someone read his blog article, he felt so ecstatic.

This website would show how many people read the article and would also show if anyone interacted with it.

Thus far, Cason had written 5 short stories and he saw one eyeball on his 4th short story.

After that story was read, Cason was officially a writer. He had skin in the game! Now he could say that he was a writer who made his writing live.

During the writing process, Cason began cultivating a rhythm.

He became best friends with his timer. The timer built the **urgency**. It made him simulate what it was like to have a gun pointed at him.

Building that urgency bulldozed through any form of overthinking. When he wrote without any care in the world, that's when he kept surprising himself.

Earlier, he thought writing was all about writing and editing at the same time.

BIG MISTAKE.

Heck, creation and editing are completely opposite in terms of strategy.

Trying to create and edit at the same time was like trying to lose weight and gain weight at the same time.

The reason why was because with creation, what was required was fearlessness and urgency.

While with editing, what was required was a timid attitude and time.

Simply understanding that there were 2 modes to writing made Cason more competent.

He wasn't quite sure where the Tales of Augusto would lead.

All he knew was that he liked writing a lot.

30

Cason went to meet up with Uncle. However, Uncle had gone fishing. It was Auntie who greeted him.

'Mr. Cason! Do you eat? Why do you look so skinny for?'

'Well, I'm waiting for an invitation for that meatloaf again!'

'I've been telling the others to invite you, haven't you been getting my messages?'

'No, I have Auntie. It's just that I've been a little busy.'

'Oooh. Busy, huh? Busy with what, a girl?'

She lightly elbowed him on the rib cage and winked at him.

'No, I wish. The main girl I met in Bahamas went back to an abusive boyfriend. I'm taking a break from dating. It's exhausting!'

'Oh no, are you okay?'

'Yes, I'm okay.'

'Cason, what you need to do is give a woman breathing room. Women are like butterflies or cats. You want to choose the analogy that works for you.'

'Huh? I don't understand either analogy. What do you mean?'

'Let's start off with a cat. When you chase a cat, what does it do?'

'It runs away.'

'But when you do your own thing, what happens?'

'The cat comes my way.'

'Exactly. Very similar with women. When you keep chasing them, you will scare them off.'

'What about the butterflies analogy?'

'There are 2 ways to get butterflies. One way is to get a net and forcefully grab them. Another way is to build a beautiful garden where the butterflies are automatically attracted to the garden. The garden represents your self-improvement, body of work, and spirit. Work on those and the right woman will come.'

'Wow! What a great analogy. Is that how Uncle got you?'

'No, your Uncle actually chased me a lot.'

'What??'

'Oh yea, the last thing your Uncle viewed me as was a butterfly or a cat. He thought I'd eventually get tired of saying no and would give him a date. He hounded me like crazy.'

'What?? I thought you were giving me those analogies because that's how Uncle attracted you?? If he didn't treat you like a butterfly or a cat and still got you, is that what you think I should do to the girl I'm interested in? I don't know much about women.'

'That's not an answer I can give you, Cason. That's something you will have to decide for yourself. You see, humans are a lot like books.'

'Oh, here we go with another analogy,' he said with a smirk.

'Seriously, think about it. A book has the physical sides. A book cover and pages. Those pages have content on them. Humans are like that. They have different skin colors and body types, aka the book covers. And they all have a different story, aka the content on the pages.'

'Hm... you make a good point.'

'When you view humans like books, it's much easier to be patient. I can't tell you whether you should treat your crush like a butterfly, a cat, or a dog because I don't know her story. But hopefully, you do. The more you know her story, the more the answers will present itself.'

'That makes sense.'

'By the way, what bought you here in the first place?'

'Well, I've been reading a couple of Uncle's books as of late. I finished the Wally book which was top notch. I wanted to get another book from the shelf in the basement if that was okay?'

'Of course.'

Auntie began walking Cason downstairs.

'Have you ever read Uncle's works Auntie?'

'I try. But your Uncle doesn't like me reading his stuff. He feels like it's too personal.'

'Too personal?? But you are his wife!'

'I know, but writers are very picky about this kind of stuff. He is not a big fan of me reading his work. It's because his work is him and a variation of him. He knows me well enough to know I can tell.'

Cason could see the logic behind that. If others could tell he was Augusto, he didn't know if he'd be able to tell as many stories without overthinking. He wanted Augusto to be filled with life. If that was going to be the case, a little privacy went a long way.

Thus far, Cason was anonymous. If he decided to stay anonymous, maybe that wouldn't be a very bad idea.

Cason looked at the library, and he grabbed a few books without looking at the names. Now was the time to read wide like Uncle had told him to.

31

As they were going to the meeting, Cason broke the silence. 'Out of curiosity Ivan, what **really** drives you to become a writer?'

'I mean I want to learn writing because I feel like it will allow me to achieve more.'

'Have you begun doing any form of writing yet?'

'Not yet. Even though Uncle says that writer's block is not a thing, for me, it feels like a thing. Anytime I stare at the blank piece of paper, I get intimidated and postpone writing. I can write when I'm forced, when a gun is facing me. But other than that, I'm not having much luck. What about you? Have you been doing any writing?'

Cason was going to bring up the short stories that he was writing on Augusto, but decided to omit that for the time being.

'Same man, I have just been doing a bit of journaling, but nothing more than that.'

The 2 finally arrived at the location to see Uncle already waiting for them.

'Today boys, we are going to do a refresher. No writing, no problem-solving exercises, and no concentration challenges. We are just going to talk.
Do you know why we are going to talk?

Ivan said:
'Because it's something that will help us refresh the information?'

'Sort of. Cason?'

'Because we are in the field of ideas?'

'Good job!! That's correct. It's because we are in the field of ideas. You guys ever heard the quote that dumb people talk about people, average people talk about events, and great people talk about ideas?'

Both nodded their heads.

'That's what we are going to do. We are going to talk about ideas.'

For the next hour, they talked about all sorts of topics ranging from politics, personalities, information theory, books, pop culture, and much more.

The topics were something that started off surface level but got deeper the more they talked.

As they were talking, it was clear that Ivan was disengaged.

'All good Ivan?' Uncle asked.

'All is good Uncle. My only problem is that it feels like we are moving too slow. I still haven't written a book like you yet. It seems like we are doing too much mindset stuff and not enough writing.'

'What you need to do Ivan is be more patient like Cason. Great ideas and building mastery requires patience and diligence.'

When Uncle said that Ivan should be more like Cason, Ivan's body language clearly shriveled up showing that he was agitated.

'I see what you are saying Uncle, but can we do a bit more writing? Because I am spending a lot of time and gas money on this. It doesn't feel like I have much to show for it.'

'Ivan, you don't have to come if you don't want to.'

Ivan sat there silently as if he was contemplating not coming anymore.

'What do you think Ivan? Are you still committed to the process or do you think you have better stuff to do?'

Ivan once again thought about it.

'You know what Ivan, you are out of here! You don't have to come anymore. Because commitment is king and you seem like you aren't as committed as you once were.'
'I am committed Uncle, but can you please begin the writing process already.'

'Let me ask you something Ivan, have you been reading like we talked about in our prior sessions?'

'No, not yet.'
'Why not?'

'Because I told you... I wanted to learn writing. Reading just seems like a distraction.'

'Ivan, you cannot create from an empty tank. Do you see what I mean? It doesn't seem like you are committed. Cason, have you been reading?'

Cason didn't want to nod his head in fear of making Ivan look bad. But he also didn't want to lie and risk showing Uncle that he wasn't committed.

So, he nodded his head.

When he said he had been reading, Uncle stopped giving much attention to Ivan for the rest of the meeting. Clearly, the 2 were fed up with each other.

What made Uncle even more impressed by Cason was that Cason had been reading Uncle's books which further showed commitment.

For the next couple of hours, Ivan became even more disengaged and showed irritated body language as if he wanted the meeting to be over.

Uncle and Cason talked.
Until the meeting came to an end.
Then he dismissed the 2.

32

'You don't want to go back to anymore meetings?'

'Nah. It's been a waste of time. I've been driving, spending time and all that with nothing to show for it. Uncle may be a great writer, but he damn well isn't a good teacher.'

Cason was tempted to disagree.

Uncle was unorthodox, but saying he was a bad teacher without applying his exercises was not fair. Uncle had a method behind the madness.

'What do you really want, Ivan?'

'I keep saying I want to become a better writer, but not going to lie... I am more curious about how to be successful. Uncle is great, but I'm going to have to find another lane. I think my problem is that I've been too focused on getting rich through writing only. I guess I'm going to try my hand at doing others things. What are you going to do now that I can't make these meetings anymore?'

Cason hadn't even thought about that. Would Uncle still accept him for the meetings or was he ready to mail it in as well?

'I'm going to have to see bro. For right now, I'm not too sure. I'll coordinate something with Uncle.'

Lowkey, Cason was happy. He felt like he could get even more of Uncle's attention and was set to improve much faster.

He did wish the best for Ivan though. Ivan had a noble goal of wanting to retire his mom. Writing was not for everyone.

Seeing Ivan faltering and wanting to quit actually made Cason *very* happy. It made him think that he was investing in a skillset with a weeding out process. Without a weeding out process, it would feel like anyone could master this skillset.

'Anyways Cason, I want you to know that you are going to get all of Uncle's attention now. I hope you use it to the best of your abilities. I have no clue what it is, but something else is driving you, I can sense it. We are still coworkers. Anything that you need, let me know and I will let you know as well.'

Ivan was talking.
Cason was brainstorming.

He was pouring with ideas.

Whenever he had an idea, it would come as a flurry of inspiration within. Now he had more stories that he could tell.

'Thank you, Ivan.'

'You want to get something to eat?'

'Nah, I'm good.'

Cason had some great ideas in his mind and he wanted to express them quickly.

33

By the time Cason came back, he was stunned to see what was on his laptop.

He saw that one of his Augusto stories had went from 1 view to 28.

As he looked at which story it was, he saw it was story number 4.

His follower count had officially risen to a staggering 5 people.

Despite the small number, Cason knew that this was the right way to go about it. He felt like there was something big that was going to come.

He began writing about Augusto going to Cuba to learn swimming. It was Augusto's dream since a little kid to learn swimming but he was too scared.

Now, he was going to be getting taught by a famous instructor in Cuba. The goal for Augusto was not to only learn how to swim, it was also to learn how to surf. He wasn't going to surf any small waves either. He was going to surf one of the largest waves that would be hitting the ocean.

Augusto would not be doing this by himself. Instead, he would be doing this challenge with a local named Carlos.

Carlos was initially enthusiastic about learning how to surf, but when he was met with conflict, his interest waned.

Carlos didn't want to learn swimming and surfing for the sake of mastering the craft. Instead, he wanted to learn it so he could impress the other people in Cuba.

So, when the going got tough, Carlos got going.

The story was pouring out of Cason.

It was a mix of knowing that others read his work and that Carlos was a depiction of Ivan. Swimming was a symbol for writing.

As he wrote, the story felt like it was being created in his mind. The words were pouring out. The punctuation, spelling, and grammar was a mess.

Anytime he was thinking about editing his writing mid-way, he reminded himself:
'Create first, then edit. **Never** combine the 2.'

Once he was done creating the story, he waited for some time.

Cason found that waiting for a few after the creation process allowed him to adjust his mind into editing mode. When he tried to edit right after creating, he'd often find himself adjusting the story too much. When he adjusted too much, that's when the flow of the story felt off.

The thing with storytelling was that it allowed the writer to see how **everything** was connected. A small detail from one line could serve as the plot twist for chapter 29.

Another thing Cason learned was the value of rules.

Before, he didn't think that creativity and rules went hand in hand. He thought the best creativity happened when there were no rules. He was mistaken. It was Uncle who helped him realize the importance of rules.

Here's why rules were so important:
- It guided the mind.

Without any rules, creativity just became chaos. With some guidelines and formulas, creativity becomes structured chaos.

After he got done creating and editing the story of Augusto's trip to Cuba, he mentally read it back. Everything flowed so well.

Upload.

After the upload, Cason thought he'd be exhausted, but that wasn't the case. Instead, he was even more curious. He began studying about writers in general.

As he was surfing through the internet, he came across an interview of a Japanese filmmaker named Akira Kurosawa.

He had never heard the name before, but decided to listen to the interview anyways.

Initially, he wasn't expecting to learn much because this guy was a screenwriter, while Cason wrote short stories.

Cason was wrong. Akira was dropping a lot of practical insights.

One of the key insights was that in order to become a great writer, you need to write a lot.

At first, Cason thought this was obvious, but it wasn't that obvious.

In the interview, Akira talked about how the professionals write even when they don't feel like it, while average people only write when they feel like it.

The main takeaway was that the professionals don't wait for inspiration. It's about writing and then feeling the inspiration later.

This was a completely reversed look of what Cason viewed as creativity.

In the interview, Akira also talked about another writer he knew that ended up publishing so much work that it would be impossible to finish reading all his content in this lifetime.

Wow!! Cason thought.

That's so much like Uncle. Uncle's written so much that it would be impossible to finish all his work in this lifetime.

Cason liked the idea.
Prolific.
What did prolific mean?

Cason Googled it.
Being prolific meant fruitful, abundant, and plentiful.

Suddenly, curiosity got the best of Cason.
What did wealth mean?

As Cason was looking through the definitions, one of the synonyms of wealth was fruitful.

Wow, so prolific and wealth meant the same thing?!

Cason would love the thought of writing so much that he became known as the Prolific Writer.

As he was thinking about it, Cason thought he could easily create a lane for himself. That could be his brand:

- The prolific writer.
  - Mr. Fruitful.

In order to be prolific though, it was necessary to write a lot now.

Not only did Akira say that great writers wrote a lot, he also talked about the importance of reading. How the modern generation doesn't read anymore. Well, you can't create from an empty tank.
Cason had no clue who the hell this guy was 29 minutes ago. Now he felt like he **knew** this Akira guy.

Cason's writing philosophy evolved:
- Don't only write what you know.
- Write what you want to know as well.

Cason spent the rest of the night reading and studying.

He pretty much lost track of time.

34

At work the next morning, Cason was feeling more excited than ever.

He was slowly starting to find his processes. After work, he was going to discuss with Uncle about the research he had done. Cason was never a big fan of studying. But now that he had a skillset that he was trying to improve, the idea of improving was becoming **addicting** to him.

Ivan called in sick.
So, it was just Cason and Ivan's mom.
It was a Sunday. On Sundays, not too many people came.

Cason liked it when it was busy because it felt like the day would fly by.

It was just him and Ivan's mom.

Normally Cason called her maam, but since they were alone together today, Ivan's mom allowed Cason to address her by her name.
'Call me Joy. Anyways Cason, how do you like making sandwiches?'

'Well Joy... you sure you want me to call you Joy? I feel a little weird calling you that. Haha.'

'Yes, that's fine Cason.'

'Well, Joy. I like it a lot. But I love writing like Uncle.'

'Oh yea? Is that what you want to do?'

'I think so. I just have no clue how I'm going to make it a thing in the future though.'

'Cason, one of the biggest qualities of a winner is to begin before you are ready. Waiting too long and thinking too much often creates cowards and takes away creativity.'

'That makes sense Joy.'

Cason felt a bit strange having a conversation with his boss. He was overly formal and wasn't in the mood to talk, but it was only the 2 of them with no work to do. Either talk or look bad to the manager.

'Hey Joy.'

'Yes Cason?'

'I just wanted to say that I'm very sorry about what happened to your husband.'

'It's okay. I made my peace with it some time back. It was tough to initially accept, but now I am okay with it. The good ones die soon but they will never be forgotten.'
Cason stood their silently not sure if she wanted to say more.

Joy continued:

'I just want you to know that in order for anyone to succeed in life, they cannot be afraid of failing. My husband had that quality of fearlessness. If he was not killed so soon, then I'm sure that he would have been able to do well for himself. Nowadays, I see that quality in Ivan. I see that quality in you too.'

'Thanks Joy.'

'I want you to guide Ivan. Serve as his brother. Guide him and give him advice.'

'Sure.'

Even though Cason said *sure*, he hadn't been acting like a brother. If he was a real brother, he would have told Ivan to keep pursuing writing rather than quitting so soon.

Also, if Cason was serving as Ivan's brother, then he would have told him about how he had been charged with drunk driving before. The same crime that took away his father's life.

35

By the time Cason went home, he immediately jumped on his laptop.
He had another story that he wanted to write.

Since the interview of the Japanese filmmaker, he had been itching to write more. He wanted to make writing a part of him like he brushed his teeth.

He opened his Word document to start his creation process.

As he was about to do that, he quickly checked to see the analytics of his short stories.

He pulled up the website with his stories.

Once he looked at the screen, he was AMAZED!!!!!!

His recent story had approximately 3,400 views.

What?
Is this a glitch?
How did he get so much views?
As he looked at the story, he saw a bunch of comments on it.

'Wow! These stories are so interesting.'
'I love Augusto.'
'This story is so relatable.'

Cason saw that his subscribers had ballooned up from 5 to 150.

Wait a minute...
How did this happen?
How did so many people see this story in the first place?

As Cason was looking through the comments, he saw that one guy had a gold checkmark next to his name.

What does the gold checkmark mean?

Cason went on the help site of the page, and saw a gold checkmark meant a premium member.

Now Cason was curious what the hell a premium member meant.

After doing some research, he saw that it meant someone who was not only a great writer, but a great contributor. These were the accounts who would scour through the site and look for stories which were not getting much love from the algorithm.

Apparently, one of the premium members found Cason's story and boosted it.

Wow, Cason thought.

He couldn't believe it.

At first, he was grateful for 3 people having read his content. But 3,400??

This was a different level.

What next?

What a dumb question.
Write more of course!!

After showing that he was capable of writing something that others wanted to read, Cason felt like he was on Cloud 9.

He began to ask:
'What can I do to write to this audience I've built up? Think!'

As he was thinking, he was overanalyzing.

Now he was feeling writer's block.

What??
Write Cason! he thought.

'What can I do to write to this audience I've built up?'

Once again, he felt stuck....

That's when once of Uncle's lessons came in:
- You write best when you're in the present.

Cason saw what was happening to him. He was getting too excited and wanted to show off to the writers. He was focusing too much on the end product.

Not only that, his mind was getting too scattered.

That's when he reframed:
'Don't write for an audience. Write for your younger self. What else would you like to tell your younger self??'

That's when Cason felt creative again.
He began writing.
And flowing.

It felt like he was the only person in the entire universe.

36

For the next couple of weeks, Augusto's popularity was skyrocketing.

He couldn't believe what was happening.
It took the initial boost to get the ball rolling.

What happened was that these stories could be read without reading the prior stories. However, it was fun to read them in a sequential order too.

The site was set up for the readers to get a diverse range of stories. Once they were introduced to Augusto, that's when they began to get curious and see if the author wrote any other stories.

One comment began showing up in a lot of the entries:
'Who the hell is the creator of Augusto??'

Cason kept getting these messages.
A part of him wanted to just change the name from anonymous and put his face and name out there.

For some reason though, he couldn't.

Often, Augusto would do something that would bring conflict upon himself. Augusto was learning the difference from strategic risks and recklessness through firsthand experience.

Cason felt that if he remained anonymous, then it would be easier to create more stories and keep the ball rolling.

He felt limitless.

Another part of him felt like the creator of Augusto should be known. Especially with this little following he built.

It wasn't just a regular following either.

Some came and went.
But there were others who became **rabid** Augusto fans.

Augusto's story had a level of relatability to it.

He was a character who wanted more, and was curious about how to experience the world.

There is this human desire deep inside that makes people want to know what else is out there. Seeing that Augusto was traveling all over the world allowed the readers to view Augusto as a conduit who would fuel their own experience.

Yes...

Cason thought in order to keep the momentum going with Augusto, it would be best not to share his identity.

Even without showing his face, Cason felt a sense of gratitude. He was learning that he was not an average writer. He was actually capable of writing stuff that others would like to consume.

He had to tell someone though.

What about Uncle?
What about Ivan?

37

Cason kept the secret to himself.

He had been having more meetings with Uncle. They talked about all sorts of things.

One day, Uncle simplified everything for him:
'You just need to write and read your writing back.'

'Wait, I need to read my writing back? You are talking about proof reading, right?'

'Yes, I mean that. But I also mean that you are to read your old writing back too.'

'Why would I read my old writing back? I don't live in the past!' Cason said in a joking and serious tone.

'The reason you need to your old writing back is because it will help you see what progress you are making. If you aren't cringing at your old writing, then you are not writing enough.'

'Geez Uncle, I wish you told me this earlier. Otherwise, I would have been reading all the writing I've been doing.'

'Have you been doing a lot of writing Cason?'

Cason was silent.

He wanted to give an update with Augusto but didn't know if he should, yet.

Actually...whatever.

He might as well tell someone.

'Yes Uncle.'

'Excellent! Do you have any of it? I would love to see it.'

'As a matter of fact, I do. You just need to promise not to tell anyone else about it.'

'Promise, huh? Wait, this seems like a big thing. Why don't you want me to tell anyone else about it?'

'Trust me Uncle, there is a reason. I just want this to be private right now. No matter what happens. I don't want you to tell **anyone**, okay?'

'Sure Cason, I promise. When can you bring your writings over?'

'Oh, we can see it right now.'

Uncle was introduced to Augusto on the internet.

Since the last time Cason checked, Augusto had gotten even more popular.

At first, Uncle didn't know what he was looking at and what the numbers, eyeballs, and likes meant. Once Cason explained it, he was caught up to speed.

Then Uncle began reading Cason's writing.

- There were some parts where Uncle laughed.
- There were other parts where he made a, 'ooo wow,' sound.
- There were other parts where he said, 'very interesting.'

Overall, it was clear that Uncle was liking what he was seeing.

Then he looked up.

'You wrote all of this Cason?

He nodded his head.

'This is great work! How did you learn to write like this?'

'I learned from you.'

Cason felt validated knowing hat Uncle liked his work. Especially because he wasn't too sure what Uncle was going to say.

'Uncle, what did you like about my work?'

'It's simple to read. It also has a profound message with a great story. You **need** to keep this series going.'

'Why do you think I **need** to keep it going?'

'Because you are going to only get better from here. Don't you see? Augusto is a lifelong character. You can keep adding to this tale *forever*. Wow! I'm just thinking about the possibilities right now. You don't know what you have at your hands right now, Cason.'

Cason thought about it...
What exactly did he have at his hands?

Before Uncle spoke further, he asked Cason:
'Why aren't you telling anyone about this? Why do you insist on keeping it a secret?'

'It's because I feel free when I write. Auntie told me how you don't like her reading your writing. She said you think it's too personal. Well, it's the same thing for me, you know?'

'I know Cason. I know that feeling very well. A true writer can be social at will, but they are often to themselves as well.'

'Right.'

'Your secret is safe with me. Now that I think about it Cason, I wished I took the same path you took. Where I didn't tell anyone about what I was going through. Being a celebrity is not good for a writer.'

'Why do you say that?'

'I say that because when you are a writer, one of the best things to do is keep the focus on the writing. However, when a writer becomes famous, they have to do other activities. They are pulled into meaningless parties, they are being asked for money by friends and family members they having talked to in ages, and they ruin their concentration skills. Remember, it's the concentration that leads to creativity. The writer's job is to keep the important thing the important thing. It's difficult to do that with too much star power.'

'Is it bad to want recognition for your work though?'

'No, not at all. If being a celebrity happens while you pursue greatness in the craft of writing, that's fine. But what I'm saying is that it's wise to avoid trying to be famous from the get go. Can you now keep a secret?'

'Of course.'

'I didn't think Ivan had the right intentions with writing. That's why I'm happy that he quit.'

'Why do you say that?' Cason had no clue why he asked that question because he already knew the answer.

'If Ivan had stumbled upon Augusto, the first thing he'd be trying to do is get recognition for it. Rather than focusing on fine-tuning his craft more, he wants to be the star of the show and be getting all the glitz and the glam. The endorsement side of things. I love Ivan, but unfortunately, his intent with writing was never about writing. It was about being a celebrity.'

'But I think he wants to be a celebrity because he wants to retire his mom, you know?' Cason wanted to make sure that Uncle didn't have the wrong perception of Ivan.

'I understand that Cason. But can I tell you something that will not be politically correct?'

'Sure.'

'To be a great writer, you need to put writing ahead of your family. Otherwise, you will top out at average at best.'

'Did you put your writing in front of your family?'

'I did in the beginning stages. But later on, my family got too big, my star power grew too much, and I lost sight of what mattered the most. Walt Disney had lost years when he forgot it was the animation that made his studio great. Papa John's lots it's way when it forgot that it was the pizza that made it great. Apple forgot its roots when Steve Jobs left and stopped innovating. The writer loses **everything** when they forget what made them great in the first place. This field is for those who are capable of being a loner if needed.'

'Uncle, that doesn't sound too pleasant to me, does it? Can't we balance?'

'You can balance, sure. But you need to define what balance is. What is it? Because if you are thinking about 50/50, that never happens in the real world. Becoming a wordsmith can make you millionaire. Heck, it can make you a billionaire. I hate when people say you don't need money to be happy. Of course you do! Money makes you *divine*. It gives you superpowers. The numbers follow the words. Master words and the money will follow. The more money you have, the more you can give it away to build more and create more. A sharp writer becomes a sharp thinker. So, when you have money in your hands, you can use it to benefit mankind. I really wished I knew that when I was younger. I didn't really maximize my potential. I think you can be a **way better** writer than me.'

'You really think so?'

'The most dangerous person to compete with is the person who doesn't compete with others. In the writing field, you win by not having a competition mindset, you win by having a concentration mindset. I think you have that Cason. I mean you have this gem of a character in Augusto, and you are not telling anyone about it! I think you respect the writing craft, and eventually, the writing craft will respect you. I guarantee you that.'

'What should I do next?'

'You become more productive. Keep working on Augusto. Eventually, Augusto is going to come **alive**. It's going to pick up a life of its own. You never know how far it can take you. Mickey Mouse changed Walt Disney's career forever. Who is to say that Augusto can't do the same for you?'

Now that Cason was thinking about it, he didn't really consider the monetization aspect at all.

Initially, he came to Bahamas to discover himself. Later, he realized that he must create himself.

Now he was realizing that a way to create himself was through the vehicle of a character that he was giving life to.

How far could Augusto go?

Cason didn't know, but he was going to stay committed to his journey to find out.

38

2 years passes.

At this stage, Cason still lives in Bahamas and is no longer staying at a hotel.

Instead, he is staying at an apartment that is right by where Uncle lives. He still works in the sandwich shop at day and is a writer by night.

His family back in Virginia is getting anxious.

'What do you mean you want to be there for another year?' Enzo asked last year.

'Trust me, dad. I need 1 more year.'

'Cason, son. Look… everyone forgot about your incident with the show. You can come back now. You have been gone for long enough. The world is not going to slow down for you, son.'

Cason didn't want the world to slow down for him.

He wanted the world to catch up to him.

At this stage, he was becoming more prolific. He released a story a week.
His release dates were almost viewed as a holiday for his fans.

His following had grown to a staggering 1.45 million online. His content had been read over a billion times in terms of sharing and all of that.

Due to the rise of global communications, Cason was able to use social media to promote his writings more.

To this day, he was anonymous.
Other than Uncle, no one else knew.

Cason felt a little cocky at times. He felt like he had stumbled into gold and transformative arts was taking full effect.

Writing was one of the most potent ways to change his perception for the best. That's exactly what was happening with Cason. Since writing Augusto, he added more depth to his own life.

This character he created had a life of its own. The more he worked on Augusto, the more he understood the character's strengths, desires, and flaws.

Sometimes, Cason felt like an Augusto to someone else's story.

Augusto felt so real!! He was like an actual person. Maybe Cason felt super real to someone else too? Maybe Cason was an Augusto to someone else's story to teach them more about themselves??

Creativity was expanding in Cason's mind. It was like he was seeing connections much better.

Not only was he seeing connections much better, random things began making more sense too. He felt like he deeply understood the quote, *'everything happens for a reason.'*

Earlier, Cason had no clue why the whole DUI Dummies thing happened to him. Nowadays, he felt like that incident happened for a reason...

What was the reason?

Without DUI Dummies, does Cason come to the Bahamas? Does he meet Auntie who would eventually lead him to Uncle?

Think about it like this...
Stories are just a series of cause and effects.

- *Because of this, this happened.*
- *Because of this, this happened.*
- *And because of this, this happened.*

What exactly was science and problem solving?

The same exact thing!
To solve a problem is to activate causation.

Causation is code for:
- *Because of this, this happened.*
- *Because of this, this happened.*
- *And because of this, this happened.*

Science and problem solving was eerily similar to a story.

Do we live in a story???

Cason discovered a few writing cheatcodes these last couple of years.

The cheatcodes that he was discovering was making Uncle a student of his.

One cheatcode was Gargantuan Thinking.

Where big general words were leveraged to activate feeling.

*I am a **flawless** storyteller.*
*I am the **greatest** writer ever.*
*I am a **trillion-dollar** wordsmith.*

The imagination didn't care about logic.

One day, Cason felt jokey and said Augusto developed x-ray vision. He would use the x-ray vision to look through women's dresses.

Sure, this was funny. Logically speaking, a person cannot possess x-ray vision with their eyes. However, simply knowing that there was an imaginative capability to do so allowed the readers to perceive that Augusto had x-ray vision.

That's what made Augusto a teacher to Cason.

Cason realized he could use words to improve this own imagination.

He would envision himself as the greatest writer ever.

Uncle was a practical guy. His systems of writing skills were safe. Practice concentration, write a lot, and read a lot.

Cason implemented those strategies along with other strategies like visualization, using grand words, and taking strategic risks with his writing.

The Cason from Bahamas was much different than the Cason from Virginia.

Nowadays, Cason had an identity.
He identified as a writer.

That's one of the reasons he needed to stay another year in the Bahamas. He felt sad telling his father that he needed another year, but he needed to make sure that his craft was the undisputed #1 in his life.

Only then could he take care of his family.

Since then, there were random people messaging Cason to see how they could 'help him' monetize Augusto.

The reason that 'help him' was in quotations is because ever since that conversation with Uncle, Cason had grown very wary of businessmen. He wanted another **artist** who was skilled in monetizing to help him monetize. Not a businessman who was going to suck the life out of the character for monetary gains.

Whatever it would take to give Augusto more life, Cason would do.

No one would take his baby away.
Cason was untrusting of most people besides Uncle and Ivan.

His relationship with Ivan hadn't faltered. Ivan found a girl to get married to so he didn't come to the sandwich shop as often.

Since his marriage, Ivan had gotten a safe job as an engineer who installed networks in other people's houses. An unusually safe job for a bold person.

Ivan lived in an apartment not too far away from Uncle.

Yesterday, Ivan invited Cason to come over and have lunch.

Cason agreed.

39

Once Cason walked into Ivan's place, he was greeted enthusiastically by his friend.

'Hey Cason!! Whatsup, how are you?'

'I'm doing well!! I bought you guys an apartment warming present.'

Cason gave Ivan 2 big sandwiches.

The 2 laughed recalling their times working together.

'Where's your wife, Ivan?'

'Oh, she works on the weekends bro. By the way, I wanted to show you something.'

Ivan had his laptop opened.

He sat Cason down and turned the laptop around.

What Cason saw made his heart drop.

He was making eye contact with the DUI Dummies video that he was featured in....

'What is this Cason?' Ivan asked. His joyous face turned stoic out of nowhere.

Cason looked back at Ivan in shock.
Wait a minute. Why did Ivan invite him to the apartment for? Was it to confront him about the video? Cason still remembered how Ivan told him how much he hated drunk drivers.

Now he was playing the video in front of Cason, with Cason clearly drunk and toppling over.

'What is this Cason? Is this why you came to the Bahamas? How come you never told me any of this?'

Cason was struggling to find the right words to express himself.

'Um...um.'

'Cason, I'm not mad at you. You don't have to be nervous. Actually, I'm just looking out for you.'

'What do you mean?'

'I now set up people's internets for a living. Bahamas is switching away from dial up and is going to get high speed internet soon. I just wanted to make you aware that there is a chance that this video gets seen by others. I just wanted to give you a heads up. I'm not going to say anything I found. But I can't guarantee that others don't say anything.'

'Does anyone else know?'

Ivan shook his head.
'What happened that night Cason?'

Cason took a deep breath and decided there was no more running away. He told Ivan exactly what caused the entire situation that night.

Cason didn't hold back any details. He talked about how he never really partied like that. How he was convinced that a girl he liked was going to be at the event that night. She never came, he got drunk. And for some reason, he decided to get behind the wheel while not being in the right state of mind.

As Cason told Ivan the story, Ivan listened quietly without any interruptions.

'Are you going to tell Uncle, Ivan?' Cason asked.

Ivan shook his head.

'I'm not going to tell anyone. You have my word. The only reason I'm telling you this is because I want you to make sure you are setting up your life in a way where you won't be destroyed if anyone finds out about this.'

For some strange reason, Cason wasn't as terrified as he thought he would be.

One of the reasons may have been because of a story that he had written about Augusto.

Cason kept that DUI Dummies episode as a storehouse of experiences that he wanted Augusto to experience.

Augusto was on the verge of settling down with his true love. But one day, he was caught drunk driving. His girlfriend's sister died during a drunk driving incident. Once she found out why Augusto was in trouble, she swiftly broke up with him.

Augusto was heartbroken.

He began crying and going down a spiral.

Days turned into weeks.
Weeks turned into months.

Augusto stopped himself before the months turned into years. That's when he invested in his self-improvement. He also began giving talks around the area on why others should not drink and drive.

Augusto added further depth to the talk by talking about losing the love of his life due to his misbehaviors.

'You don't have to physically take a life away to experience the loss of a loved one,' Augusto would say.

That line from Augusto's talks struck a nerve. It had multiple people spreading news of Augusto. Events were desperately trying to book him.

Soon, Augusto's former girlfriend got wind of this story. When she found out how Augusto used his dark experience to inspire the new generation to take a different path, she was touched.

She contacted Augusto.

When Augusto saw her and how she had grown more beautiful, he became ecstatic.

She wanted to give him another chance.
Augusto cleaned up his act and got back together with her.

This was the short story that propelled Cason's following. This short story was shared so much that Cason was flooded with even more business inquiries.

The reason that this piece was important for Augusto and his fans was because it showed how things in life come in full circle.

Cason didn't know when, but one day, he was going to say: 'I'm so happy that DUI Dummies happened.'

He had no clue when that day was going to arrive, but he had the **faith** that day would arrive.

This is why when Ivan found the video, Cason was scared, but not too scared. He was more terrified at the idea of losing Ivan as a friend.

Now he didn't care too much about the event. Ivan telling him how he knew, but would keep it a secret touched Cason. Cason decided he would now share a secret with him too.

'Can I tell you something Ivan?'

'You can tell me anything Cason. We are best friends. Or at least I consider you my best friend.'

Cason hadn't ever thought about the concept of a best friend before. Now that he thought about it, it made sense that Ivan was his best friend.

'Thank you, Ivan. I want to show you Augusto....'

40

When Ivan heard about Augusto, he didn't see what the big deal was.

But the more that Cason gave the numbers that Augusto was pulling, the more that Ivan's eyes were glowing.

Cason even logged into Ivan's laptop to show the direct messages that he was getting from well-known businessmen.

'Caffeine Cooper hit you up?? You know he owns the most famous publishing company in all of Bahamas, right??' Ivan asked in excitement.

Cason didn't know that, but he wouldn't have been too surprised.

As Ivan saw the numbers that Augusto was pulling, he had to ask:

'Cason, why the fuck are you anonymous? You should be showing your face to everyone. You could have merchandizing, movies, and comic books made! Cason trust me, you aren't thinking big enough with this man. You literarily have a goldmine!!!!"

'I know that Ivan. But here's the problem... I don't want to be a celebrity. I talked to Uncle about this. He said too much fame is not a good thing for a writer. A writer is best when they keep their craft as #1.'

'With all due respect Cason, but Uncle doesn't know what he's talking about. He's a great writer, but a poor businessman. He never realized what it took to make the dollars flow to him. I think that philosophy of keeping the writing number 1 is selfish. You should write to get rich so others around you can do well.'

Cason thought Ivan had a good point.

Sure, getting rich was not a bad thing as long as he did it the right way. However, Cason didn't want to sacrifice the quality of Augusto to get rich. All these comic book strips, merchandising, and products could come later. Right now, Cason preferred to perfect his craft.

'I see what you are saying Ivan. I am not one of those artists who thinks money is the root of all evil, trust me. But I think I may have gotten a little lucky with Augusto too soon. I think I need a bit more time to fine tune Augusto some more. You know what I mean?'

From Ivan's facial gestures, it was obvious that he didn't know what Cason meant. However, he wasn't going to argue with his friend.

'Look Cason, I don't know the direction you want to take this. But I just want you to know that you did well.'

'I did?'

'Yes. Since those training days with Uncle, you have done well. I didn't take the writing thing as seriously as you did. You had concentration skills while I didn't. I just wanted to say, great job, my friend.'

'Ivan, thank you so much. I just wanted to say that I miss you at the sandwich shop because I felt like we built a strong bond really quick. You are my best friend too. Thanks so much for bringing up the DUI Dummies thing to me. Thanks even more for keeping it a secret. And thanks even more for supporting me with the direction of Augusto.'

'Alright bro, before you thank me even more, just give me a hug... Because I got good news.'

'What Ivan?'

'I'm about to be a father.'

Surprised, Cason got up and gave Ivan a big hug.

'Wow bro!! I can't believe it! Congratulations man.'

'Thanks Cason. Hopefully you got familiar with this apartment, because it's going to be your last time seeing it.'

'It is?'

'Yes, I'm moving out of the Bahamas.'

'You are???'

'Yes. Bahamas served us well, but it's time to raise my kid somewhere else. I'm moving to Florida or Texas.'

'Wow Ivan, I'm really going to miss you. Are we still going to stay in touch?'

'Of course. You are going to be my son's Godfather.'

'I am??'

'Yes, you are. Don't worry, I'll get you updated with all the details soon. For the time being, I just want us to talk about the good ole' days. I miss being single and a person without any worries. Now I worry a lot.'

'You do? Why?'

'You are single Cason, so you won't know. But when you have a wife and a kid on the way, there's a lot more at stake, you know? I don't really have time to focus on myself like I used to. Nowadays, I'm either just working or thinking about going to work. I thought at this point, I was going to have a business that worked for me. But it looks like the 40 hours a week grind is going to be my destiny. You need to take risks to start a business. With a baby on the way, the last thing I can do is takes risks. That's why you are in the best position to succeed. I really hope you make the most out of this. Especially before you get married and have kids yourself.'

'I will make the most out of this Ivan. Thanks for believing in me and making me the Godfather. Any idea when you're moving?'
'Yes, tomorrow.'

41

The conversation with Ivan went great. Eventually, his wife came home. That's how long Cason was there.

Cason shared entertaining stories of all their sandwich days together. Ivan's wife was pretty, very soft spoken, and seemed like someone who had to put in a lot of hours at her job. She looked exhausted once Cason saw her.

Cason really hoped that Ivan was going to one day be able to make his business passion work. Seeing Ivan working as an engineer was definitely a few levels up from making sandwiches. However, Uncle and Cason both knew Ivan. They knew that this wouldn't last too long.

Cason and Uncle met up for another late-night meeting.

The 2 were consistently trading tips with each other.

Once Cason walked into Uncle's basement, Uncle was already waiting for him, writing by hand.

'Do you write everything by hand?'
'I do. That's why you will die more prolific than me.'

'What?'

'You can type much faster than I can write. I tried the whole typing thing, but all it would do was hurt my head. When you are in pain, it's difficult to be in creation mode. Creativity happens when you are in the zone. Sometimes, it's wise to put yourself through some physical discomfort to build creativity. Who knows, I may try picking up typing like you.'

Cason never really thought about that. He wrote some journals by hand. But the idea of writing an entire book by hand seemed like a challenge that he did not want to participate in.

'You wrote all those books by hand??'

Uncle nodded.

This man was prolific. Now the prolific writer was telling Cason that he would be more prolific than him?

'How was your meeting with Ivan?'

'It went great.'

'Did he tell you about the move?'

'Oh, you already know??"

'Of course. How was your interaction together?'

'It went well. I told him about Augusto.'

'You did what??'

'I told him about Augusto. I thought he should know. Especially because we have had so much training together.

'I thought you were going to keep this anonymous, Cason?'

'I was. I mean I've only told you and Ivan so far.'

'Yes, *so far*. Who are you going to tell tomorrow? Your brother, your mom, then your dad? This was supposed to be a goddamn secret Cason!!'

Uncle was getting furious.
Cason was shocked.

'Hey Uncle, relax. I only told Ivan. I'm not going to tell my mom or dad. Not even my brother. You don't have to worry Uncle.'

'Cason, that's how it begins. You break one promise with yourself, and chances are you'll break another one soon. I really wished you kept this anonymous for the time being. You still have so much work to do.'

'What do you mean? I know I have more work to do, but you are making it seem like I should be embarrassed showing my face for the work that I have done.'

'No, that's not what I'm saying. All I'm saying is that you have done great work, but you're still not emotionally ready for too much exposure.'

Thus far, Cason had viewed Uncle as the staple of truth. However, today...he didn't agree with Uncle.

'I think you're overthinking this Uncle. Clearly what I'm doing is working. I decided to stay anonymous out of my own will. But that doesn't mean if I show my face, I'm going to be disgracing anyone, especially myself. Augusto is my creation, and this creation has impacted lives for the best.'

What Uncle was saying was not too far from what Cason was saying. He viewed Cason as a great writer in the making. However, he wanted to make sure that Cason wasn't taken advantage of.

'Sit down Cason.'

He sat down.

Uncle began speaking.

'A few decades back, I was in a position very similar to yours. The book *Wally* that you read was one of my first fiction books. Although I liked it, I didn't love it.'

'Why not?''

'Because it was altered.'

'Altered how?'

'The true story lines were warped by the publishing company so they could sex it up.'

'Sex it up?'

'Yes, so they could market it better. Being a naive guy as a youngster, I let these people who had no writing experience, alter my work. They made it more mainstream and cookie cutter.'

'What do you mean? That was the first book of yours I read and I thought it was nothing short of amazing. You did a fantastic job with that book!'

'If you think that book was amazing, then read this.'

Uncle went in his cabinet and got a large stack of papers with hand writing on it.

'I present to you, the original Wally.'

Cason grabbed it and observed it.
This man really does write everything by hand!

'Can I take this home and read it?'

Uncle nodded his head and continued speaking.

'What I didn't know back then was that a lot of these publishing companies don't care about the story first. They care about maximizing their profits first. So, they will alter the author's work and change the direction of their career. I want to make sure what happened to me doesn't happen to you.'

'What exactly happened to you Uncle? I mean, you became one of the most prolific writers of this generation. It seems like you did well for yourself.'

'Did I? Look at his place!'

'What do you mean?'

'I wrote the stories and these publishers paid me pennies. I make it seem like I am against business and capitalism at times, but I'm not. I got played Cason. I am the most prolific writer of all time, but I don't even own the rights to my library. My publishing team does. I should have built more leverage. Or who knows, mastered my craft even more so I could have been self-published and built my empire on my own.'

'Who cares Uncle? I feel like you are overthinking this. You may have made pennies, but you sold a lot. Everyone in Bahamas knows you. You aren't a money guy either, so that's all good. You are an amazing writer.'

'I know I'm not a money guy. But I could have had more control if I didn't give away power of my career so quick. I just want you to avoid giving away your power so fast. These suits are going to come to you and try to hypnotize you with sign in bonuses, a free car, and all these commercials. It's easy to sign away your control. I just want you to have so much faith in yourself that signing away your library is viewed as a joke.'

Cason was listening to Uncle.
Uncle wasn't talking about the money.

He was talking about controlling your destiny.

'I now see what you're saying Uncle. You know what, it was a mistake on my end to tell Ivan. I shouldn't have told anyone, but I'm glad I told you. If I didn't tell you, then I'm sure I wouldn't have known a lot of the things I know now. Especially about control. Maybe Ivan may drop a few gems along the way too?'

'Maybe Cason. Please be careful. The world is hungry for content. When they see quality content, these corporations do **everything** to turn the artist into a packing mule. I know you are better than that. I want you to be better than me. I want you to understand the words and numbers of our business.'

'I'm a sponge. I will learn whatever I need to learn to make you proud.'

42

The conversation with Uncle went great. Heck, he was happy that Uncle confronted him.

Cason had a very blurry vision early on, but nowadays, he was evolving his vision some more. It was not enough to just write, Cason had to understand the business side of things as well.

From the product, all the way to the sales page, to the accounting side of things.
This would allow Cason to have more control over his destiny.

Without the confrontation, Cason would have never prioritized the importance of control.

Now he knew he was going to make sure Augusto was kept a secret until he had more confidence in himself.

What is confidence?

On Google, confidence is defined as clarity. Someone with supreme clarity does not need to pretend to be someone they are not. Instead, they could just be themselves and be confident for it.

In order for Cason to build confidence in himself, he needed more competence. Writing alone wasn't going to be enough. He needed the writing to fuel his vision.

Some of the best visions are often secrets. The creator says one thing to the public while they have another thing solely for themselves.

Right now, Cason was using Augusto to make himself great.

Every experience, trauma, and setback that Cason was facing in his life could be channeled into Augusto. Not only were the dark moments channeled into Augusto... Augusto would absorb the dark parts and turn it into light!!

Without Augusto, Cason doubted he would have made peace with the DUI Dummies incident. But once he channeled that experience into Augusto and was able to create an ending with a lesson at the end, that's when Cason's perception regarding the event had changed.

There is a famous quote that says:
'Change the way you look at things and the things you look at change.'

Cason experienced that.

He always gave others great advice. His friends and family back home would often ask him for advice because he was good at problem solving for them.

But when it came to his own life, he did a a poor job in solving problems.

Why?

Because when we try to solve our own problems, the ego has the tendency to get in the way.

The ego blinds the person and finger points to avoid taking accountability.
Therefore, one of the best things to do was write out the problems.
Earlier, Cason wasn't sure if writing was a portal towards problem-solving. Writing while creating another character like Augusto was not only a portal towards supreme problem-solving skills, but it was also a portal towards supreme imagination.

43

Cason drew inspiration from so many places. The restaurant business taught him how to sell his future books. Listening skills taught him about other people's perspectives that he could eventually write about in his own tales. His own conflicts created beautiful story topics that could be expressed in the narrative format.

After thinking about it for some time, Cason was planning his trip back to Virginia. He didn't know if he was going to tell his parents and brother about it, or if it should be a surprise. All he knew was he learned a lot in Bahamas.

Cason looked different.
His face had more character than it once had. Before, he was a straight up baby face with little to no definition. Nothing stood out.

Nowadays, Cason had grown his midnight shadow and had a more chiseled, matured, and artistic face. The gym was not his thing. Other than eating 1 sandwich a day, he didn't get much calories. This gave Cason a sharp jaw line.

Every now and then, some cute girls would come to sandwich shop and flirt with Cason. They'd say:
'You can make my sandwich any time.'

Cason's manager, Joy, would often egg them on and talk about how Cason was single. After they would leave, Joy would be like:
'Cason, you should talk to them. You are one of the most sought-after bachelors in the Bahamas.'

That was clearly a lie.

Despite Cason looking much better than before, it was clear that he was not a ladies man. But he had a writer's charm.

Since writing, he didn't ramble as much. Often, writers are very well spoken. It's because they are great with words and know how to get to the point.

Despite him knowing that other girls liked him, his heart still belonged to Brooke. How weird! He barely knew her but he kept convincing himself that she was his love.

What was love?

He'd often write about love in his stories of Augusto.

One day, when he was writing uninterrupted, one of the definitions of love came up:
When you enjoy someone despite their dualities.

Which meant that in order to love someone, it was about accepting their good **and** bad sides.

Along with Brooke, the main things he loved were his parents, brother, and Augusto.

His parents and brother were obvious, but Augusto was strange. This was something that was not even real! How could he love this character so much?

He loved the character so much because Augusto was Cason. He had seen Augusto go from unconfident to confident to a much more nuanced personality.

Augusto meant so much to Cason.

What made Cason's writing very thought provoking was that it was not meant to only be entertainment. Augusto was educational as well.

There was one direct message he received from a children's book publisher who asked if Cason would think about making an Augusto edition for kids. The lessons from these stories would have an impact on children.

As of late, the politicians had politicized kids books. Augusto could shed truth for all walks of children while maintaining authenticity.

Cason liked the idea of a kid's edition of Augusto, but he didn't love it.

He liked the idea because he could see his creation making an impact on the youth.

He didn't love the idea because he felt that creating strictly for the youth would dilute Augusto. He wanted Augusto to experience life and the gritty sides of it.

There was *massive potential* for his creation.

The follower count for Augusto had ballooned to 12 million people!!!

The day he was ready to release a book, he'd be an instant millionaire.

The monetization opportunities excited Cason, but what excited him even more was mastering the craft of writing.

Thus far, Cason had learned from so many industries. One of the industries that he didn't expect to learn from was electrical engineering.

Because an engineer is trained to hide his work. Which meant that he needed to hide the guts of the circuit.

A user of a remote controller does not want to see the wires and batteries sticking out. They want to have no clue what is going on inside. They just want to use the remote.

For Cason's writing, no one could know how messy his writing looked at the initial stages.

It was so messy without any semblance of clarity. To an outsider, they would have viewed it as gibberish. To Cason, it was a **puzzle**.

By editing his own work, Cason felt like he was solving the puzzle of himself.

Because what was writing?
It was simply frozen thoughts.

By the time Cason was editing his own work, he began analyzing his mind. Saying:
This should have been there.
This entire section can be eliminated.
These words can be switched around.

After editing his own work, he was thinking clearer than ever. How could other writers not edit their own work??

Did they not see the opportunities they were missing out on?

It was a beautiful process of:
Entropy to art.

The world would be hidden of the messiness that goes behind the creative process.

However, Cason would always know.

44

Cason woke up from sleep.
This morning was different.
He had a sensation in his stomach that made him think something was wrong.

'What is wrong?? Am I hungry?'

No, Cason never ate breakfast.

'Is everything okay with my family?'

He called his family and everyone was okay.

'Was everything okay with Uncle and his family?'

He called Uncle and his family and everything was okay.

Then what the hell was going on??

He had no clue.
Best to not overthink.
It's probably just one of those gut sensations that comes which doesn't mean anything.

But for Cason, his gut instincts had been one of the conduits of his creativity.

If he was feeling so strange, there must have been a reason, right?

Well, he checked and no one seemed to be under any harm. He was definitely overthinking this.

He went about his day.
He went to work.
Worked for hours.
Dealt with the good customers & the bad customers.

Later, he met up with Uncle and discussed writing.

Then he had dinner with Uncle and his family. Auntie felt extra talkative.

Joy was quiet. She was probably sad that her son moved out of the Bahamas with his wife.

Everything was going well on the outside. Still, Cason felt like something was off.

Why??

No clue.
He didn't tell anyone about this problem.

After dinner, he walked back home. He looked at the stars as he was walking back and everything still looked normal from the outside.

Aha!

He knew what was going to happen.
It was time to give Augusto a new challenge.

The challenge of when intuition and intellect don't agree with each other.

Sort of like what Cason was going through today. Intellectually, nothing was wrong. Intuitively, he felt like something was wrong.

Maybe he could morph this dilemma into a story that would teach others a thing or 2 about when the head and heart fight.

The idea captivated him.
I can't wait to write this piece!!

As he finally got home, the feeling had gotten worse.

Normally, he did a bit of reading before he did his writing. Since he was so frantic, he had no clue if he would be able to sit still and read. He decided to go straight into writing.

Was everything okay with Augusto?

It felt like something had happened to Augusto.
By the time he opened his laptop, his worse fears were confirmed.

45

As Cason opened his laptop, he could see that someone had been in his account. The last login showed a time that Cason was away.

What the hell??
How was he hacked?

Not only was he hacked, his terrible gut feeling began getting worse as he started looking at his messages.

Someone was talking to the publishers that wanted to work with the anonymous writer.

'Of course, I would like to roll out a kid's version. What are your ideas?'

'Of course, we can begin a cartoon series.'

'Absolutely, I'd love to come on the show to do a face reveal today.'

What??
Face reveal?

Cason became terrified. His work with Augusto was in jeopardy and he had no clue who to call for help.

He couldn't call a support team because he was anonymous and didn't want to risk showing his face or saying his name.

What was he supposed to do?
His heartbeat was racing...

Augusto.
No...
Please don't let anything happen to Augusto.

Cason began feeling weak. He heard about artists getting their ideas stolen before, but he never thought it would happen to him. Sure, it may happen if he was showing his face to the world, but that wasn't even the case...he had been private.

How could something like this happen to him?
Why did bad stuff always happen to him?

Cason began pacing around the room.
What was he going to do?

He began reading the different messages.
One of the messages stuck out:
'Absolutely, I'd love to come on the show to do a face reveal today.'

Today??

He checked for the time.
The time of the show that this hacker was supposed to speak at was 11 pm.

It was 11:23 pm.

The show had already begun.

Cason hurriedly found the station that he was supposed to tune into.

He clicked the hyperlink.
The show started mid conversation.

Cason looked at the hacker on the screen speaking with the utmost confidence.

Cason's heart dropped.
He was certain that he wouldn't recognize the hacker.

But as had watched the hacker take credit for Augusto,
Cason was proven wrong.
He knew this guy very well.

The hacker was Ivan....

46

Cason was at a state of shock as he saw Ivan getting interviewed as the creator of Augusto. Giving his candid responses and lying through his teeth.

'Well, when inspiration hits you, you just strike. That's what happened with Augusto. I was taking a shower and the idea just flashed before my eyes,' Ivan said with charm.

Cason became furious.
In the shower? You got to be kidding me!

'What are the future plans for Augusto, Ivan? What do you plan to do with this?' the host asked.

Ivan's smirk turned into a full-blown smile. He had been waiting for that question.

'The plan is to turn Augusto into an **empire**. We are going to be selling Augusto books, shirts, comic books, movies and so much more. This is going to be the modern-day Mickey Mouse. You can bet your ass on that.'

The interviewer was in awe of Ivan's business mind.

'So Ivan, why now? You have been anonymous this entire time. Why decide to show your face now?'

This was the question that seemed to have stumped the lying Ivan. He thought about it, then gave his response:
'I felt like it was time. There is only so much I can do while being anonymous. For Augusto to grow, I need to think big and put a face to the brand. This is my life's work and I don't see any harm in being recognized for my work.'

Cason's fist clenched.

He was furious.

It was his life's work? What the fuck was wrong with this guy?

He should have seen this from a mile away. Uncle was right. He should have kept Augusto a secret. That must have been why Uncle freaked out so much when he heard that Cason told Ivan about Augusto. Uncle was probably aware of Ivan's intentions all along.

Cason felt weak as callers began calling into the show asking Ivan questions about Augusto. Surprisingly, Ivan answered the questions without stumbling.

Cason was almost certain that when questions regarding Augusto came, Ivan would stumble and be proven as a fraud. But that wasn't the case. Instead, Ivan was answering these questions like he really was the creator of Augusto.

It was clear that he was no dummy.
He had a sharp business mind who did his homework before coming on the show.

Cason's clenched fist softened.

What a betrayal. Why??

Since coming to the Bahamas, he had never done anything to Ivan that was in bad intent.

Cason couldn't decide which was worse:
His DUI Dummies appearance or losing Augusto to this snake.

He couldn't move.
He began feeling dizzy.

Suddenly, Cason slammed the laptop on the floor.

It shattered.

Then Cason began crying because Augusto was no longer his....

47

7 years passes.

At this point, Cason moved back to the United States.

He was back in Virginia as if the Bahamas trip never happened.

His mom, dad, and brother all took him back with open arms.

Each of their empires had grown since Cason's Bahamas trip.

Nowadays, Enzo was one of the most sought-after criminal lawyers in the United States.
His mom had grown her fashion empire into a symbol rather than just a business. Wearing a dress was no longer considered archaic, it was considered cool.

Billy was officially a millionaire.

They were surprised to see how Cason hadn't changed much. They thought he would be taking more risks after his Bahamas trip.

However, Cason seemed more like a loser now. After taking the strategic risk of letting Ivan know about Augusto, Cason was left with a poor taste in his mouth. He was no longer a strategic risk type of person.

It would be much better to be a behind the scenes guy.

Even though Cason wasn't being logical, it was clear that a bitter attitude was washing over him.

Losing Augusto was similar to losing a son. His passion for creative writing had dwindled.

Every now and then, his brother would look to hire content writers for one of his many business. Cason would think:

Why hire content writers when you can hire me? Do you know that your brother is the creator of Augusto?

What made Cason's heart drop was when he saw his mom reading a book of Augusto.

'Where did you get that mom?'

'Where did I get this book? It's in Barnes and Noble. You should read this Cason. This Augusto guy truly is breathtaking.'

Cason became furious.
He was the creator!
Nowadays, it would show Ivan Smith as the author.

Ivan went onto become what he always wanted to become:

A wealthy man.

Ivan was clearly media trained. He was the type of guy who could easily fool the public into thinking Augusto was his.

The act of writing became repulsive to Cason.

He still kept in touch with his crew from Bahamas. Most specifically Uncle.

Uncle would often have talks with him where he would say: 'Listen up Cason, I promise you will feel better if you keep writing. Don't give up so easily.'

The conversation would turn south when creative writing was bought up. The last thing Cason wanted was a lecture.

Cason was heartbroken.
He wasn't doing much with his life.

He was 34 years old.
Didn't have a girlfriend.
Didn't have dreams.
And was the odd one out in his royal family.

Despite others forgetting about the DUI Dummies stint, Cason felt like a bigger loser now than he did back then.

48

'Cason, what the fuck is wrong with you?' asked Billy.

Billy was 35 years old, had a wife and 2 kids. He lived very close to the house that him and Cason had grown up in. Almost walking distance.

'Huh, what do you mean?'

'I mean, what did you move to Bahamas for in the first place? Remember a while back you were going to go to the Bahamas in order to change yourself for the best? Can I be real with you?'

'Yea...'

'You are a bigger loser now than you were before. And you are making this entire family look bad!'

Cason was crushed hearing his brother talk to him like this, but he didn't have enough confidence to fight back. All he could do was stay silent.

'I mean, nothing changed with you Cason. You literally go to the Bahamas and come back without **any** fire. No promotions, no progression, no life, no family, no kids. Nothing man. A fucking loser!'

Normally, Billy was kind towards Cason. Seeing Billy's sudden vitriol was out of the ordinary.

'Look, I'm telling you this because I heard mom and dad worrying about you nonstop when you were in the Bahamas. What kept them going was how they thought you were going to turn your life around after the DUI Dummies incident. But you made your life even worse now than you did back then. You really need to grow the fuck up.'

Cason just sat there silently listening to his brother's tirade.

Although Billy had moved out, Cason was still living with his parents. The same room that he always lived in.

It's like the years were piling on, but the transition from a child to adult was not happening for Cason.

He had gained a lot of weight since returning.

Before, he was a skinny nobody.
Now he was a fat nobody.

'Tell me something Cason, what did you do in the Bahamas? Did you just go there and stay in your room the entire time?'

'No Billy.'

'Then?'

'I worked in a sandwich shop.'

'Besides the sandwich shop, what else did you do? I find it surprising that you were there for so long and didn't invest in any skills or meet a girl. Come on man, be hungrier.'

Cason wanted to be open, but the idea of him telling his brother that he invested in a skill and a girl, then lost both of them did not sit right with him.

'I know Billy, you're right.'

'You're back to the same job you had before you left. Do you even like accounting?'

Cason shook his head.

'Then?'

'Then nothing Billy. What do you want me to say?? I am a loser. I ruined my life. I knew it back then when I was on TV and I know it now. You don't have to keep reminding me!'

There was an awkward silence in the room.

A silence that spoke volumes.

Billy went on to break the silence.

'Now what Cason? What do you want to do? I think mom and dad are too kind to you. Maybe they like you living in this big mansion of theirs so they don't have to be empty nest parents. I need you to know that I'm not trying to put you down.

Instead, I'm trying to get you to become the best version of yourself. I really want to see you win.'

Cason could hear the tone from Billy's voice. The aggression had melted into concern.

Billy really did want Cason to succeed.

Thus far, his parents hadn't reprimanded him too much since the whole ordeal. That was because they wanted him to stay home.

So, it was Billy who had to give him a reality check.

Billy would never backstab him like that piece of shit Ivan.

If it were not for Ivan, Cason's life would be on a completely different track.
Cason would have mastered the craft of writing and would have learned the business side of things.

Wait a minute...
The business side of things.

What makes Cason think that he would have effortlessly walked into business?

He watched a lot of documentaries of athletes who came into business thinking they were going to succeed, only to fall flat on their face.

Just because he dominated in one field did not mean that he would dominate another.

'What do you want me to do Billy?'

'I want you to strive for more Cason.'

Wait, maybe this was happening for a reason.

Since writing so many of the stories for Augusto, Cason's mind learned to think in cause and effect:
- Things often happened for a reason.

Even though his storytelling mind had been buried away in shame and self-pity, Billy's aggression was a wake-up call to awaken Cason's inner artist.

If Cason would have put Augusto in this scenario, what would Augusto have done?

The answer was obvious!
Augusto would have already mastered writing. Therefore, now he would want to learn the craft of business. Augusto would sneak advice from the same person that was giving him a scolding at the moment.

'Billy, I need your help.'

Billy could automatically sense a different tone from his brother. As if he just got a brilliant idea.

'Yea Cason, what do you need help with? I'll be more than willing to help.'
'I want to learn business from you. I will work for free. Whatever you need for your businesses, I will do it. Grunt work and all of that.'

Cason recalled how intense his writing sessions with Uncle was. Billy couldn't be that bad.

Billy was waiting for the moment when his brother would be interested in business. He knew that his brother viewed business as a mechanism for the greedy capitalists to make money.

Billy used to view business like that in the beginning stages. He did what every business owner did in the beginning. He asked:
'How can I make more money?'

And all decisions stemmed from that narrative.

This poor narrative is weeded out painfully.

Eventually, all business owners make the transition of:
'How can I make more money?' -> 'How can I provide more value?'

Provide more value and the money is inevitable.

That was the reason for Billy's growing empire. It was because he altered his thinking from being selfish to selfless.

Nowadays, he viewed business as an art.

He would teach his brother the correct way to do good business.

Business is a mental sport. It doesn't matter how old you are or how much of a loser you think you are. At any stage, if the desire is strong enough, then business can be learned.

Before Billy was going to take Cason on as an apprentice, he was going to test Cason's desire.

'Cason, I would love for you to join my businesses.'

'Awesome, thank you so much Billy.'

'But...'

'But?'

'But I want to know that you have desire in this. How do I know you are serious about this? How do I know that you aren't going to quit? Just because you are my brother does not mean that I'm going to go easy on you. If you want to learn, then you **need** desire. Thus far in your life, you haven't proven that you have the desire to keep pushing on even when your back is against the wall.'

Strangely, Cason felt somewhat relieved by this challenge. That meant that Cason wasn't going to be getting coddled by his brother.

Now, he felt the same FIRE he felt when Uncle began challenging him.

Cason composed himself, then said:

'Listen Billy. So far in my life, I have proven to be a loser. My life has been a cautionary tale of what *not* to do. But when you run away from problems, problems find you. Problems always find me and I shrivel up. You on the other hand have always been different.'

Billy was listening.

'This entire family has greatness that I don't. Mom is a visionary, dad is a dog, and you are creative like none other. I need to make my presence felt. I'm 34 and have nothing to show for my life. Please don't let the rest of my life be a mess too Billy. Without you, I don't know if I will be able to turn this around.'

It crushed Billy to see his brother so helpless as an adult. When they were kids, it was Cason who was the smart one. That brother who was once voted to be the most successful was now one of the biggest losers he knew.

Not if Billy could help it.

He was going to help Cason turn his story around.

'Okay Cason, I will teach you everything I know.'

49

Cason felt a new surge of enthusiasm that he hadn't felt in a long time. The enthusiasm he felt was the enthusiasm of learning.

To show Billy that he was serious, he bought a bunch of business books. One of the business books was by Josh Kaufman, the author of the Personal MBA.

This book was a very practical look into business in a language that everyone could understand.

The book bought up the core human desires:

1. The desire to protect.
2. The desire to bond.
3. The desire to know.
4. The desire to acquire.
5. The desire to defend.

Number 3 was something that was sticking out to Cason. It's like when curiosity was on his side, he was **unstoppable.**

The same curiosity that allowed him to learn writing at rapid rates would be the same curiosity that would allow him to learn business.

Curiosity made focus feel like light work.

The first couple of meetings with Billy was beginner's stuff. He walked him through all the businesses he had.

His businesses ranged from selling tumblers, to compressions gear, to selling Bluetooth beanies and much more.

Cason was in awe of how Billy was able to do so many things. How was he able to run so many different businesses? Curiosity got the best of him.

'Billy, how are you able to run so many different businesses? Don't you ever feel confused?'

Billy smirked.
He could tell that Cason wasn't just showing up. He could tell that his brother wanted to **know**. This was a hyper targeted question that showed Cason's desire.

'To the outside world, it seems like I'm doing a lot. But in my world, I'm only doing **one** thing. I need you to think in themes.'

Themes?? Cason thought. Why would a businessman possibly think in themes for? He thought that's how writers thought.

'Themes, Billy?'

'Yes. Poor business owners are asking, what product or service can I get to make money? Great business owners think, how can I provide useful value to my customers?'

'What does this theme help you do?'

'It simplifies my thinking and decision making. It allows me to empathize. **All** the products that are under my business empire are here for a reason. It's here because it providing useful value to a bundle of people. From providing useful value, all other things take care of themselves.'

'Can you give me an example?'

'Sure.'

Billy pulled up one of his businesses where he sold stainless steel tumblers. What a bland business. How could anyone want these??

When Cason learned this business generated $100,000+ in profits a year, he was in awe.

'Cason, don't you hate it when your coffee gets cold or when your soda gets warm?'

'Yes, I do.'

'Wouldn't it be great if you could keep your coffee hot and your soda cold?'

'Yes.'

'Well, that's what these tumblers are for. It gives the useful value by allowing the customer to have a pleasant drinking experience. When thinking business, think human experiences. And when thinking human experiences, think in pleasure or pain.'

Wow!

Cason just got another analogy with writing.

First, Billy was telling Cason to think in themes. Cason would think in themes right before he would begin writing. He would ask himself, *what is the gist of this piece?*

The second insight was just as compelling. To think in human experience, think pleasure or pain.

Since creating stories, Cason viewed himself as the speaker of human experiences.

That's why others loved Augusto so much. Because Augusto was relatable.

To make Augusto relatable to others, he would often be involved in plots which had pleasure or pain.

Sometimes, everything was going well with Augusto and he could do no wrong.

Pleasure.

Other times, in the same story, everything was going wrong for Augusto and he could do not right.

Pain.

That dance of pleasure and pain was what storytelling was all about!

Was Billy saying that it was the same with business? That the customers only viewed things in pleasure or pain?

'I see what you are saying Billy. What about all the other stuff that makes business seem so complex? You know...all those funnels, trackers, numbers, split testing and all that. Are you saying those aren't as important?'

'Those are important. Think about it like this Cason... Can you proofread an essay without any content?'

Cason enthusiastically shook his head sensing another business to writing analogy was coming.

'Exactly. It's the content that is king. But let's say that the content has typos, bad grammar and all that. Well, then the secondary important thing is proofreading. Now imagine if we living in a bizarre world where the experts place more importance on proofreading than the actual content! How silly would that be? Everything would feel so much more complex. Similarly, it's the same thing with businesses. A lot of these so-called experts get you so focused on the proofreading versus actually creating the content! They want you to focus on all these details before even providing any value!! That's why they overcomplicate business.'

Cason's mind was blown.

He couldn't believe his brother viewed so many concepts of business in the exact way a writer viewed their writing.

Cason began to think this was too much of a coincidence.

Once again, Cason felt like he was living in a story. He felt like the Augusto to a Cason-like storyteller. Because no way did strange coincidences like this happen!!!

How random was it that his brother was capable of so fluently merging business and writing?

It was time to worry about that later.
For the time being, he knew with Billy's guidance, he would be able to learn business in a way that MBAs and renowned entrepreneurs couldn't even fathom.

50

Training with Billy was very similar to training with Uncle. Billy was hard headed and strict with time.

If you were on time, that meant you were late. If you were early, that meant you were on time.

The training conducted by Billy was so polished.

Growing up, there was a certain period that teachers and the guidance counselors viewed Billy as a dumb kid. Someone who wasn't going to amount to much.

But they were dead wrong about him.

Billy was too gifted for school.
Billy was a street smarts guy who was capable of seeing through the lines.

That's what made him great.

'You need to take your fatass to the gym by the way, Cason.'

Billy jokingly tapped Cason's stomach.

'I know I'm fat right now. But what does that have to do with business?'

'Business is a mental sport. It's one of those things where you learn firsthand that the body has an effect on the mind. You are pretty much problem solving and thinking. That's business in a nutshell. Try problem solving and doing business when you are out of shape. You may be okay in doses. But over time, you will get tired. Start going to the gym.'

Cason nodded his head.

'What questions do you have for me Cason?'

Whenever Billy asked Cason that question, it was translation for:
'Ask good questions. Show me that you have been learning things on your own.'

'Have you noticed a stunning similarity between business and writing, Billy?'

The question caught Billy off guard.
Normally, Billy was used to thinking in numbers. Why the random angle with words? This got Billy's curiosity.

'Hm, no I haven't noticed a similarity, why do you ask?'

'I want to tell you a secret that I haven't told anyone in the US. Can you promise to keep it a secret? I am asking because something happened to me in the Bahamas that traumatized me from telling others about secrets.'
Billy nodded his head.

'You promise Billy? You can't even tell your wife.'

Once again Billy nodded his head and said:
'Yes Cason, I promise.'

Cason took a deep breath.
'So, I began learning writing skills while I was in the Bahamas. I began training with a pretty esteemed writer. He taught me a lot. He taught me to think in themes, how to problem solve, and provide value through content. Thus far, since you've been talking about your business, I keep getting reminded of my writing classes. I just wanted to see if you were seeing a similarity with writing and business as well.'

The 2 talked more.

This time, Billy began questioning Cason. He had no clue that his brother was well versed with writing. If that was the case, Billy would have assigned him as a content writer from the very beginning.

Cason wasn't aware of how coveted his skill was.

After talking about their ideas of writing and business, Billy eventually asked:
'Cason, what is the status of your writing skills nowadays?'

'I mean, I don't do it anymore. That's something I used to do when I was in the Bahamas.'

'Why did you quit?'

'There was someone who stole one of my grandest ideas. That just turned me off to writing. I don't want to talk too much about that if that's okay.'

'Look Cason, you are sitting on a gold mine of a skillset and you are too unaware to realize it.'

'What?'

'Physical real estate is built from cement, wood, and glass. Digital real estate is built from ideas, concepts, and stories. Cason, you have one of the most coveted skillsets out there to build a digital empire!! Why aren't you sharpening this skillset more?? You know what?? No more free classes. I will **only** teach you business if you promise to teach me everything you know about writing.'

'Everything?'

'Everything!!!'

Cason did not see himself as a teacher by any means. But if he was going to be forced to teach his brother, then sure.

'Writers **thrive** in the internet age Cason. Nowadays, there are social media apps to promote your writing. It's easier than ever to become self-published. Do you think you are rusty?'

'Yea, I'm rusty.'

'How about this...There are a couple of thousands of people coming to my sites. Why don't you try writing some content for those sites to take the rust off?'
'You really mean that Billy?'

Billy thought about it. He was paying ghost writers for average quality work. Why not get his brother to do it for free?

He wasn't too sure if his brother was a great writer, but something in Billy's gut told him that Cason would prove to be special.

51

For the next few weeks, Cason didn't only show his greatness with writing.
He showed his greatness *and* efficiency with writing.

Where it would take Billy's ghost writers 1 whole week to turn in an article, Cason was capable of doing it in 1 hour.

Cason's writing was breathtaking.
Simple.
Informative.
And funny as hell.

'Cason, when the hell did you learn to write like this? How do you get your writing done so fast? I never saw such quality at record speed.'

Cason began teaching Billy about the difference between creating and editing.

He explained to Billy that when you create, you need to be fast and move with urgency. Understand that everything will make sense once you are complete. For editing, you want to be precise and observant.

The problem with most writers, and most likely Billy's ghost writers, was that they try to create and edit at the same time.

Billy was a note taker. He would take notes when Cason talked about writing.

Billy was in awe of his brother's skillset. He couldn't believe that his brother didn't use his skillset to build a library of books!!

Cason felt different when he was teaching vs when he was being taught. Nowadays, he assumed the role of Uncle.

Teaching someone writing allowed him to understand the craft of writing from different angles. He was often asked questions by Billy that he was not expecting.

'How am I supposed to create characters who think and have identities, Cason?'

What a simple question.

'Well Billy, you don't want to reinvent the wheel. Assume we are living in a story. Imagine all the people you know. What are their identities like? How do they talk like? What are their dreams and desires? Well, get those same characters and slap a different name on them. Just like art imitates life, often, life imitates art.'
Billy couldn't believe how wise his brother was. He was definitely going to take this to the bank.

The 2 brothers had a brilliant idea.

They were going to create a character for one of Billy's businesses and tell stories. The character would have a personality, problems to deal with and would also subtly promote the products.

Just like McDonald's had Ronald McDonald, Billy needed ideas for his business.

Without hesitation, Cason delivered the golden idea that would soon make both brothers supremely rich.

'Let's start off with your tumbler business first. *Tumbler Tom*, it's simple. I can create stories on that.'

Billy's heart bounced in excitement. What a simple name. And from seeing his brother's writing, he knew that something sensational was going to happen.

Billy was wrong.
Something sensational didn't just happen.

Something legendary happened.

Cason began chugging out stories of Tumbler Tom.

His first story was about how Tumbler Tom's brother died from rust. At first, the rust was not noticeable because the tumblers were painted over. Later on, the rust began to ruin the quality. Once the quality diminished over time, that's when the tumbler began to diminish over time.

After the loss of a loved one, Tumbler Tom promised that he would ensure tumblers had the highest quality steel that was not prone to rust at rapid rates.

That's when Tumbler Tom would promote the tumblers that were sold by Billy's company.

The idea was so brilliant.

The simple blog began to get shared all over social media. The tumblers *soared* in sales.

'Cason, you are a gifted, man! You know your blog on Tumbler Tom's origin story of losing his brother made a bunch of people cry?

'Cry in a good way or a bad way?'

'In a good way Cason!! When your products can make someone **feel** a certain way, that's when you have them hooked. Look at all these comments talking about how much they love Tumbler Tom. Cason, you don't know how big this is. Can you create 20 more blogs for me?'

Without hesitation, Cason created 20 more blogs.

Each blog was riveting.

Tumbler Tom met different characters.
Had different challenges.
Each blog had a unique way of promoting the tumblers sold by the business.

The blogs were so riveting that the content didn't even seem like promotional pieces anymore. These seemed like entertainment first, and selling later.

What was the phrase?
Story selling…

Billy couldn't believe what he was witnessing. Initially, he hired Cason to just shadow him. Nowadays, Cason was tripling his profits and turning his products into market leaders.

Being the high integrity businessman Billy was, he immediately began cutting Cason checks. He was not going to get such high-quality work for free.

The first time he gave Cason a check for $2,500, Cason grabbed it and began crying.

Billy was shocked by the reaction.
'What's wrong Cason? Is this too little? I'll give higher checks over time. We are just beginning.'

Cason notified Billy that he wasn't crying because the check was too little. He was crying because he felt like he was paid too much.

He never knew that he would make money with his writing one day.
Cason continued crying. Then he said:
'I **really** needed a win…that's why I got so emotional man. Thanks for the check.'

Billy couldn't believe that Cason didn't see what he saw.

'Cason, I don't think you see what I'm seeing. You are a STAR with writing. You are a wordsmith. Your quickness and imagination will make you a superstar man. I... I....I want you to be my business partner, Cason.'

Cason couldn't believe what he was hearing. Was he really selling himself short? And did his brother really want to go to business with him?

For the longest, Billy wanted Cason to be interested in business and this was the first time that Cason was actually showing interest. Not just a little interest, but a lot of interest.

The $2,500 check was enough to turn the whimsical fantasies of writing into a reality.

He normally got paid that in 2 weeks for something he hated in accounting. Would this really be possible?

Billy had an empire of brands.
Who was to say that Cason couldn't create a version of Tumbler Tom for each brand?

The ideas were going through Cason's mind right now.

Waldo the Wallet.
Billy Bluetooth.
Cameron the Camera.
Cason looked at Billy.
'Brother, I would **love** to go to business with you.'

52

Billy and Cason's partnership was a match made in heaven.

Billy would focus on the business side of things that dealt with money management, hiring, and product research.

The *only* thing that Cason was responsible for was the creation of the stories.

Creative writing was his **only** priority.

Not only did he write short blogs for the businesses anymore. Nowadays, it had ballooned into something much bigger.

The characters from the businesses had developed a cult like following.

The characters of Tumbler Tom, Billy Bluetooth, Cameron the Camera were given their own shows on YouTube.

This was a **masterclass** on content marketing. The 2 brothers became quite the celebrities in the content marketing space.

With the rise of the internet, a lot of marketing became borderline scammy and cringe. There were so many ads, popups, banners, and garbage posts.

Both Billy and Cason had a philosophy in mind. **Everything** would be built on content marketing. The stories would be all that was needed in order to promote the business.

Not a dime in ad revenue.
The money saved on ad costs were all reinvested into the expansion of the business.

This was very similar to what Sam Walton, the founder of Walmart, did to build his empire.

Rather than focus so much on targeting the big cities like Kmart and Target, Sam Walton focused on the small towns instead.

The reason that this strategy was genius was because he saved a ton of money on marketing.

When one the locals of the small town went to the store that sold everything, the very first thing they would do was tell all their friends. That allowed the organic rise of the Walmart brands. The money saved was reinvested into the expansion of Walmart.

This was the exact philosophy that Billy and Cason shared.

The 2 were becoming known as content marketing specialists.

There was major interest in their business model from the Financial Daily news organization (a mainstream news outlet that dealt with finances, business, and investing topics). They requested an interview with the 2 brothers.

The 2 brothers accepted.

During the interview, the interviewer bought up Cason's past of being on DUI Dummies. The interviewer thought she could get a story by putting Cason in an embarrassing spot. She even replayed the clip of him being drunk and crying.

She asked if he would do anything differently?

Billy was clearly frustrated by the question and was looking at Cason like:
'If you want to walk out, then I'll walk out with you.'

But Cason didn't react negatively.
He said:
'Do you know how much pain I felt after that moment? I was traumatized, couldn't eat and felt like my life was over.'

The interviewer listened.

Then Cason looked directly at the camera.

'To anyone who is going through a tough time right now...keep going. Don't hurt yourself, don't put yourself down, don't run away. Instead, embrace **all** of that pain. Eventually, the pain will be used to propel you towards something that you never deemed possible. The darkest moment of my life eventually turned into the best moment of my life.'

That small snippet allowed Cason to go from being a creative writer into something much more. He was seen as a redemption story of what it was like to turn from a disgrace to a hero.

Nowadays, Cason looked back at that past embarrassing moment with joy. He needed that event to humble him.

Never get too proud.
That was the mantra that Cason followed.

Since the building of the characters, Cason and Billy worked out an idea to have the characters collaborate with one another.

Tumbler Tom would go on adventures with Waldo the Wallet.

The blogs which developed into shows eventually developed into movies.

The content was not only entertainment, it was educational as well. The 2 brothers were not only pioneering content marketing, they were also pioneering in edutainment as well.

Others tried to copy their strategy.

Companies were not even trying to hide their plagiarism.

They created 'Tumbler Timmy' to promote their tumblers.

So similar.
It even looked like Tumbler Tom!

There was a period where Tumbler Timmy was making a mockery of Tumbler Tom. Tom would appear in Timmy's content being portrayed as a fool and an inferior quality product.

Old school Cason would have been heartbroken that he was being stolen from again. But this time, he recalled one of Uncle's lessons:

- Concentration.

So, he began to concentrating.

Other knockoffs emerged, but no one seemed to have the magic that the 2 brothers had.

Even though Billy was getting a lot of credit, he knew that without Cason, the business would not have **magic**.

It's like Billy had set up the skeleton of the business prior to Cason's arrival.
But it was Cason who poured life into that skeleton.

The sky was the limit for Cason!!

His newfound success showed him that a career can be transformed once the desire is there.

His newfound success also bought back some old faces.

One of those old faces was Brooke.

53

As Cason was going for his morning run, he saw Brooke waiting outside of his house.

When he saw her, he became flustered. He was not expecting to see her. He was not expecting her to even know where he lived.

When he greeted her with a formal hello, she gave him a tight hug like she had missed him. Like she wished that she didn't leave with her ex and had taken the strategic risk with Cason instead.

The 2 went to a coffee shop like the good old days.

'How have you been Cason? I saw that Financial Daily did a special on you. From the background of your interview, I could tell that you were in Virginia. I just moved here recently and thought it would be nice to visit you.'

The feeling of love he had for Brooke had not melted one bit.

But their relationship was no longer the same.

Brooke had 2 children with her ex. She was single at the moment. Just like Cason had predicted, her husband thought he was too good for her and left her.

Although Cason loved Brooke, he knew that they did not have a future. Or at least, that's what he thought.

'What do you think Cason? Do you think we can ever give it a shot?'

Cason was silent.
'We'll talk about that later Brooke. Anyways, how has everything been?'

He was postponing the answer to see more of what Brooke was about.

He didn't really know Brooke nowadays. This wasn't Forest Gump where he was going to center his whole life around this woman. A few years back, she had the opportunity to give him a chance, and then she proceeded to go the other way.

Cason had created a bunch of stories that had the theme of: *Fool me once, shame on you. Fool me twice, shame on me.*

Now he was being given a difficult decision.

'I have had a tough couple of years Cason, not going to lie. You were right when you said that I shouldn't have given my boyfriend a chance. He was very judgmental. After I had our 2 kids, I was constantly scolded by him for having gained so much weight. I did the best that I could for being a mom. It eventually got so bad that I found out that asshole was having an affair with his secretary. He got so angry that I found out that he left me for her.'

As Cason listened, he could tell that Brooke had been living in hell. She was not that same joyous girl that she had been in the Bahamas. She still had beauty, but nowadays, she was carrying a lot of guilt.

Despite Cason wanting to give it another chance, he knew it was not the right time.

She spent most of the interaction complaining. She didn't seem as curious about Cason as she once was. Rather, she was using him as an opportunity to vent and express her frustrations.

As a creator, it's the mental health that matters the most. When the mental health is in jeopardy, that's when everything else is in jeopardy.

Younger Cason wanted to fix others.
Nowadays, he wanted to offer them the chance to fix themselves.

'With all due respect Brooke, we are at completely different stages of our life right now. I want the best for you, but I cannot be with you.'

Before Brooke could cry and try to convince him otherwise, he said:
'Although I cannot be with you, I want to help you.'

That's when he pulled out a blank check from his backpack and wrote it for $13,000.

'I hope this will help you and your family.'

In Cason's mind, that was the initial reason she came. She didn't want to be with Cason. She wanted resources for her kids, especially after being made a single woman.

When he handed her the check for $13,000, she began crying uncontrollably.

The same tears that Cason shed when he was given his first $2,500 check by his brother.

They often say that money cannot buy happiness. They were wrong.

Money can buy happiness when you give it away.

Cason was secretly very rich. He built his empire through words. His business model was simple:

- Turn words -> numbers

Numbers were simply the byproduct of the words he produced. The words were simply the byproduct of the thoughts he produced.

At a fundamental level, money was just an idea.

Cason wasn't just writing Brooke a check...
He was giving her the idea of hope, happiness, and freedom in the making. He was giving her some peace so she could sleep comfortably without waking up mid-way in the night worrying about unpaid bills.

The pain that Cason had felt these past few years had given him a lot of empathy for other people's pain.
Some may judge him for giving this girl who rejected him in the past so much money. But nowadays, he simply didn't care.

Cason became wealthy to change his perception and help others along the way.

Just like he never needed credit for creating Augusto, he didn't need credit for being a Robin Hood who created his own wealth and gave it to the needy.

Cason needed to have his character challenged to grow as a person.

As he saw Brooke crying uncontrollably after seeing the check...he only realized that he needed to invest more in creative writing.

He was now a wordsmith.

His words really had the power to change someone's life forever.

54

As for Ivan, things had changed.
Eventually, the cat came out of the bag.

In the initial stages, Augusto had seen massive success. Shoe deals, comic book deals, movie deals, and much more.

The money came flooding in.
Overnight, Ivan was a millionaire.

He was shocked that Cason never came gunning for him. Sure, he ended up moving, but with the internet, it wouldn't have been too difficult to find him.

Ivan won the battle.
But lost the war.

Nowadays, running the Augusto company was becoming draining. He was consistently dealing with backlash for the poor-quality work, was having difficulty paying his workers, and was losing his sense of self.

Although he was a good businessman, he was far from **great**.

One thing that Ivan learned since stealing Augusto was that a business could not be a one hit wonder. Great businesses had to be rooted in lifelong innovation.

Ivan was never the writer that Cason was.

Results?

Cason was making a splash right now and it was Ivan who was struggling.

Ivan had been made aware of Cason's recent success from his wife and son.

They had both bought items such as wallets and glasses. What was crazy about the simple items was the **awe** that it generated.

'Dad, you won't believe it! I bought Georgie the Glass!!'

'Georgie the Glass? Looks like a regular glass, son. Why are you calling it Georgie for?'

That's when Ivan's wife broke down what made this glass different from all other types of glasses.

It was a glass with a story.

Ivan's son bought his laptop to him and started playing a dramedy to Ivan. A mix of a drama and a comedy.

Ivan was witnessing content marketing like he had never seen in his entire life.

It was a beautifully produced show of a glass looking to fill itself up. The more it tried to fill itself up, the more it struggled.

The story taught Georgie the Glass that it was not meant to fill itself up, instead, it was meant to be of service to a human. The glass needed to cleanse its ego and quit trying to do everything by itself. Once that happened, Georgie became of service to a human. The human would provide the glass with a home and utility & Georgie would finally be filled up.

The video wrapped up with how to buy the Georgie the Glass.

Then he saw:
Story written by Cason Stratton.

Wow!
He was taking his creative writing skillset to the bank.

In a world where there were incessant marketing messages, this brand was bringing people towards them.

The problem was that the brand was scattered. It sold a bunch of different products. Products ranged from glasses, to wallets, to tumblers and much more.

Each of the products had a story that bought it to life to the customer. Still, everything felt so scattered.

How awesome would it be if the content and the products were united under one brand?

What Cason and his brother were doing was **phenomenal**. There company was a blend of Disney and Amazon.

Ivan wished he didn't place short term profits over long term thinking. That's what made Cason different than him.

Cason always wanted to master the craft of writing. He wasn't so profits oriented like Ivan was. However, in the long run...it was Cason who was winning.

It would be an honor if they could collaborate again like back in the days. Like when they were working in the sandwich shop, going to Uncle's secret hideout, and problem solving together.

Ivan didn't mean to steal the Augusto idea. He just saw that Cason had logged into his computer and never logged out.

He saw all the direct messages from the top writers, publishers, and celebrities in the messages.

This was years ago.

He was more mature now than the money hungry Ivan of the past. Especially since he had a son. He was not going to teach his son to be a short-term thinker. He was going to teach his son to be a long-term thinker.

He wanted his son to be like Cason.

A long-term orientated kid who could make decisions that were creative and filled with concentration.

It hurt Ivan knowing that his business was in shambles and that Cason was going to the top with the proper decision making.

Luckily for Ivan, he was getting offers to sell the Augusto brand. It was not chump change either. He was being offered millions of dollars from high end investors who were chomping at the bits to own the assets of Augusto.

Despite the brands poor sales as of late, a business titan or a creative superstar would still be able to turn the company around.

Why not both a business titan and a creative superstar?

The more Ivan thought about it...

The more he was having his decision made for him.

55

'You know boys, you 2 are like Yin and Yang.'

Mom was looking at her 2 sons, proud.

Billy and Cason had grown from boys to men. They were what any mom would want from their children. The 2 boys were close, collaborating, and bringing honor to the family name.

It warmed her heart seeing her baby boy, Cason, finally standing on his 2 legs. He was a symbol of how you should never give up. Anytime she needed strength to fight her own battles, she would recall what a warrior spirit Cason had cultivated throughout the ages.

'What do you mean we are like Yin and Yang?' asked Cason.

She said:
'Study the greats, sons. You'll see that businesses are often broken down into 2 qualities. The analytical and the creative. It was like that with Walt and Roy Disney. Walt was the creative powerhouse while Roy was responsible for taking care of the finances and numbers. Look at Steve Jobs and Steve Wozniak. Jobs was the creative big picture thinker and

Wozniak made the products come to life with his detail mindedness. Word is spreading fast, sons. You 2 are being viewed as the modern version of that. You guys are impacting **all** industries. The big businesses began resting on their laurels. But your innovative business is changing everything up. No will view business the same way again after my sons are done with it.'

Cason looked at Billy.
Billy looked at Cason.

Cason was so happy that Billy had given him that wakeup call. Without it, he may have still been stuck in a rut doing something he had no business doing.

What Cason really admired about Billy was his analytical mind. His ability to do market research, find products that the market would want, and create systems.

Billy looked at Cason admiringly as well. He was astonished by what a magician his brother was. Billy had never seen a creative force like Cason. Not only was the kid prolific, he would routinely create gripping narratives that challenged the mind and tugged at the heart.

Based on what Billy was doing before, he was going to be a millionaire at most. With his partnership with his brother, there was no denying that they were on the road to becoming billionaires.

Their business's most unique selling point was the breathtaking stories that Cason told.

That's what would prevent others from copying them. Cason wasn't copying anyone, he was truly innovating.

Since Cason came into the business, sales were not only tripling, they were 10xing!!!!

There was one thing that was holding the business back from being great. Everything was too scattered.

Decentralization is great.
Because it's hard to take down a business which has a solid decentralization plan.

However, the problem was that truly great businesses had the capability of being decentralized and centralized.
Which meant the products could be from all over a variety of markets, but could be united under 1 brand.

Unity underlying the multiplicity.

What would be the name of the brand?

The 2 had no clue.
There was nothing that quite stuck.

By finding a unique name, they could become one of the greatest businesses of this generation.

What made the story even more compelling was that the 2 head honchos were brothers.

The media loved how the brothers brought their unique talent stack.

Cason was happy with what had happened. His skillset was designed for him to only get better with time. He only had to focus on *one thing*:

- Keep getting better at writing.

The amount of characters he bought to life was building his confidence.

Despite the massive levels of confidence, there was still one thing that was eating away at him...

Augusto.

It crushed him to see what Augusto had become. The character of Augusto had become corporate. Nowadays, he was just a walking billboard for other companies to market off.

The story lines lacked any semblance of depth. Nothing was thought provoking.

Augusto lost his identity.

If Cason was given one more chance to take ownership of Augusto, then he would be the happiest man alive.

Cason had set up 4 piggy banks for his money:

- 25% would go to expenses. This was what he could spend.
- 25% would go to investing.
- 25% would go to an emergency fund which he wouldn't touch unless of an emergency.

- And the final 25% would go to donations.

Cason had been a Secret Santa for a lot of people. He loved the idea of doing things anonymously.

Maybe it was to recreate the feeling of when he was anonymously writing Augusto's stories.

Routinely, Cason would hear stories of people in need and he would write a secret check to them.

The last time he did something like that was when he heard a mom who was unable to afford her daughter's operation. He was eavesdropping in the conversation. Afterwards, he followed her to the hospital where her daughter was staying in.

Cason went to the nurse and said that he would pay the woman's fees. Apparently, she didn't have insurance either.

The price would come out to 84,328$.

The nurse was shocked when he said he would pay the *entire* thing. She was even more shocked when he wrote the check right in front of her! She was the most shocked when he gave the nurse $10,000 dollars to not disclose his face or name.

He sat in the lobby pretending to read a newspaper.

The nurse told the woman that a good Samaritan would be paying for all her hospital bills.

At first, the mom couldn't process what happened. When the information finally clicked, she broke down crying and thanking God.

That made a dent in Cason's heart.

Not only did it make a dent in Cason's heart, it **fueled** his mind. The more he strategically gave away to causes to better impact other people's lives, the more he had ideas.

There may have been a reason for that.

There are 2 philosophies regarding a human.

- They are inherently sinful.
- Or, they are inherently pure, but are covered with ignorance.

Cason loved the latter philosophy. He could also visualize it.

He was cleaning his dirty plate once. The plate was so dirty that it was almost unrecognizable.

It would have been incorrect to say that the plate was always dirty. It would have been wiser to say that the plate was naturally clean, and it was temporarily dirty. In order to make it clean again, you needed to scrub away the dirt.

Likewise, Cason began to view himself as a flawless storyteller. He felt like he was already one of the greatest creators of all time. However, he was ignorant of the fact.

In order to clean his plate, he would strategically give away money to make other people's lives better.

Cason learned this lesson the hard way though....

When he was getting a lot of money, he tracked down the information of the producer who placed him on DUI Dummies. Then Cason made it the effort to make his life a living **hell**. He hired people to leave mean comments on his family's social medias, call in death threats, slash his tires, and much worse.

Cason didn't stop there.

He wanted the entire DUI Dummies show cancelled. He threatened the executives that if the show was not cancelled, then Cason's company would not do any form of content creation for their other shows.

Media companies sought out Cason's creative writing prowess for some of their own shows. He quickly proved to be an amazing screenwriter who could produce hits quickly. Cason was a coveted ghost writer for many studios.

However, if they kept DUI Dummies on air, then Cason would not write **anything** for them.

After Cason's ultimatum, the network producers quickly cancelled DUI Dummies.

Getting revenge felt SOOOO good.

He felt like he finally avenged his younger self. The feeling was great!!

But the feeling eventually faded.

Eventually, he felt like his plate was dirty and it was harder to be creative. After showing poor intent towards others, Cason learned that if he wanted to be the greatest writer to ever exist, he needed to make sure that his mind was pure.

For his mind to be made pure, the piggy bank he invested the most attention in was the donations piggy bank.

He learned his lesson that revenge was not worth it. While he was going to be on this planet, he would ensure that his writing, his creations, and his actions were making others people's lives better.

Not worse.

56

'Hey Cason?'

'What Billy?'

'There's a guy who wants to see you. I know I normally try to insulate you from all these advertisers and agents, but this guy said he knew you from the Bahamas.'

'Yea? Who is he?'

'Ivan.'

Ivan?? No way! Cason thought.

Cason told Billy to invite him in.

Ivan walked in with a hesitant smile on his face. He had clearly gained some weight and his eyes seemed like he hadn't slept in ages.

Ivan was not too sure how Cason would react to his unexpected visit. He didn't know if Cason was going to even shake his hand.

Cason smiled at Billy letting him know that he was good to head out. When Billy left the room, Cason's face turned to business as usual.

'Hey Cason? Remember me?'

Cason nodded his head.

He was trying to be a good person and make other people's lives better, but all he wanted to do was make Ivan's life a **living hell**. He took Cason's beloved creation and destroyed it.

It's like someone kidnaps your son, turns your son into a scumbag, and then tries to make small talk with you.

'Yes, I remember you. I have not forgotten a thing. We didn't end in the best of terms.'

It was crazy how the tables had turned. Nowadays, Cason had bought fitness into his life and cleaned up very nicely. While Ivan seemed like he was drowning for the past couple of years. Clearly, he bit off more than he could chew.

'Cason, before we begin, I believe I owe you an apology. I just wanted to say from the bottom of my heart, I am so sorry for stealing from you. I do not expect you to forgive me. I do believe I should apologize while I'm here because I have been keeping up with your success.'

Cason was listening to every word Ivan was saying without interrupting him.

'I just wanted to say...you were right. You always were right, Cason.'

'Right about what?'

'You were right in terms of your attitude. When Uncle was teaching us writing, you were paying attention. You were embodying everything that he was teaching. Like how to be present in the moment, take strategic risks, and you were actually writing. I was just listening and thinking about how I was going to get rich.'

Cason nodded his head, feeling somewhat appreciative that Ivan was giving him some recognition. But it was not enough to erase the distaste that he held towards Ivan for the betrayal.

'I'm so sorry Cason. When you left my house that day, I just panicked. I was making pennies at my job. I was actually on the verge of getting fired. And my knees were shaking about being.... being a father Cason. I'm so sorry. I messed up and broke your trust.'

Cason never thought about why Ivan stole from him like that. He always assumed it was to make more money. He wasn't aware that that it had anything to do with his son.

'I just messed up Cason. I'm so sorry. I'm sure you are aware of the current state of Augusto?'

Cason nodded his head with a disgusted look on his face.
'I'm so sorry for letting your creation get to this state. I will give you *all* the royalties that I have gotten in the past couple years. That royalties come out 250 million dollars.'

Ivan put the check on Cason's desk.

Wow....
250 million dollars?
That was a **staggering** amount of money.

Despite Ivan having stolen from him in the past, making amends with this much money showed that he was serious about repairing the friendship with Cason.

But Cason didn't feel good about the money. Especially by how it was obtained.

'I'm good, Ivan. I don't want the money.'

Ivan looked shocked.
He was sure that Cason would go running for the money and everything would be forgotten. But what a stupid thought that was. Cason was an artist at the core. The money was a means to an end, but *never* the end.

After seeing Cason's sad face, Ivan quickly thought on his feet.

'And...'

He was thinking of something. He wasn't sure if this would work, but it was the only thing he could think of.

'And, I would like to give you Augusto back. I have tons of investors looking to buy it from me. But I would like to give you **your** creation back free of charge.'

Cason sparked up like there was a lightning rod that hit him.

He had no clue that he could be given the rights back to Augusto. To this day, Cason didn't know too much about the legal sides of business. He was sure that since Augusto had gone corporate, that getting the rights back would be impossible.

'You… you can do that, Ivan?'

Seeing Cason's sudden shift in body language, Ivan knew this was what it would take to make amends with Cason.

'Yes Cason, I can do that. I will do that. I will give **all** the rights of Augusto back to you.'

Ivan was shocked that Cason was still interested in Augusto. Especially since what Augusto had devolved into.

This just further highlighted the amount of love that Cason had for Augusto.

'Yes Ivan, if you want to do right by me, then just give me full rights back to Augusto, you can keep this.'

He gave the 250 million dollar check back to Ivan.

Ivan looked back at Cason, puzzled. What an intriguing figure this guy was. He really was not motivated by the money at all. He really was an artist. No wonder he had excelled so much.

Cason couldn't believe that he was going to be reunited with Augusto. His skin was feeling tingling sensations and he was at a loss for words.

He had waited so long to have Augusto back. Nowadays, Cason was a different man. He would bring Augusto to life… that was his promise to himself.

Ivan looked at Cason.
'Hey Cason, can I suggest something? If not, no worries.'

Thus far, Ivan had ran Augusto to the ground. Why would Cason listen to any of Ivan's suggestions? But something in Cason's gut told him to listen.

'Sure.'

'I've been following very closely to what you and Billy have been doing. And honestly, I am amazed at what you 2 have been able to do. But…'

'But?'

'But everything is too scattered. I don't think you understand the powerhouse of what you 2 have at your disposal. How about uniting all your different products and content under one identity? My wife and son bought products from your brand recently. But when they bought it, they both knew your business by a different name. How about uniting it under one name?'
'Yes, Billy and I were thinking about it. But we have been unable to think of a name. You got any ideas?'

'Well…how about Augusto?'

Suddenly, Cason felt adrenaline.
The hair on his skin rose up.
And he felt a chill down his spine.

This was it!!!
Augusto.

Ivan continued.
'Amazon has 6 letters. Disney has 6 letters. When I think of your brand, I think of a hybrid of Amazon and Disney. So, 7 letters will do the trick in my opinion. Augusto can be the brand ambassador like the gecko from the Geico commercials. If you hate the idea, no worries. I was just thinking about it when I was coming here.'

Cason was at a loss for words.
Ivan was right!!
Augusto.

It was so simple.
So elegant.

'Ivan...'

Ivan looked at Cason as he was about to get shut down.

'Ivan, I LOVE the idea. Thank you so much for giving me this idea.'
Ivan was surprised that Cason loved the idea. He was expecting to be shot down. He was even more surprised when Cason reached towards him for a hug.

The 2 hugged in silence.

Since the past couple of years, Cason had been struggling for an identity. He traveled to the Bahamas trying to find that identity.

Later, he learned that he didn't just find an identity.

He needed to create an identity.

The creation never ended.
It was a work in progress.

Mankind is a work in progress.
Ivan messed up.

But Ivan coming back and owning up to his mistakes like a man was something that Cason could forgive. Ivan too was a work in progress.

The 2 hugged and there was a strong chance the friendship could be salvaged.

57

Auntie was on life support.

When Ivan told Cason about the situation, he was going to take a trip back to the Bahamas with a colossal check in hand. He would do **anything** to make sure that Auntie did not pass away.

Without her, none of this would be possible.

She was the sweet woman who introduced him to the Bob Marley shirt, gave him food, and introduced him to a new world.

Without her love on the opening night of Bahamas, there was no saying what Cason would have done. Maybe he would have just stayed in his room the entire time.

Since the interaction with Ivan, Cason talked to Billy about centralizing the brand under one name.

When Cason told Billy about Augusto, his eyes lit up. Even though Billy was a logical guy, he didn't need any market research to understand that this was a brilliant idea.

Cason would make his announcement of being the original creator of Augusto. That would be enough to set the world on *fire.*

The same guy who created Waldo the Wallet, Georgie the Glass, and Tumbler Tom was the creator of Augusto??

Unbelievable!

To make sure that Ivan didn't look bad, Cason would also announce that due to lack of finances, he gave permission to Ivan to come out as the originator of Augusto. Cason liked his lowkey lifestyle and didn't want to be in the spotlight. He would ensure that Ivan didn't face any backlash for stealing the character and running it into the ground.

Cason would bring Augusto back to the top.

Since Ivan came into their inner circle, he had been bubbling with business ideas. Since he was an outsider, he was able to give Billy and Cason advice from the lens of a consumer.

One of the most breathtaking ideas?

Create Augusto Land.

This would be very similar to Disneyland. However, Augusto Land would be on an actual island by itself. Tourists would come to interact with their favorite creations. There would be shows, movies, hotels and much more on this island. Ownership 101. Heck, the cruise ship that bought the tourists to the island would even be owned by Billy and Cason!

The idea was so brilliant that Billy and Cason were really thinking about making Ivan a 3rd partner. But Ivan wanted to prove his integrity first. He said he would simply come on as a consultant until both brothers could trust him.

Having a son really changed Ivan. He wanted to make sure he never took shortcuts again.

The question was...where would they build Augusto Land?

They knew the answer.

They would buy an island right by the Bahamas. Tourists from the Bahamas would be able to sneak a trip to Augusto Land as well.

When the announcement was made, the world went on a frenzy.

The announcement of the brand being known as Augusto was a gamechanger. It was enough to centralize the brand and give it the identity that it needed.

Augusto had grown.

Once Cason got Augusto back, he wasted no time created plots and storylines that bought the depth and richness of Augusto to life.
No one would ever understand Cason's true secret for creative writing.

The secret was that he would use bits of himself on the characters, so the characters would give him more perspective.

The more stories Cason wrote, the more his dirty plate became clean. The more that his dirty plate became clean, the more he realized that he lived in a story.

He wasn't even just saying this in a poetic sense. He truly believed that he lived in a story.

Human experiences had pain and pleasure like a story.
Human experiences dealt with characters like a story.
And quantum physics talked about the observer effect. How a particle would turn from a quantum soup of possibilities to a particle only once the information was taken.

Sound familiar?
Sounds like a book.

When a book sat in front of a reader, untouched, it was just a quantum soup of possibilities to the human being.

But once the book was cracked open and read, that's when the energy waves turned into particles.

Cason learned that he lived in a story from the stories that he created.

Every character.
From the wallets.
To the coffee mugs.
To the big towers.

All were born from Cason's mind.

He loved writing.

Writing gave him a new way to look at reality.

He had more money than ever. The simple business plan never changed:

- Turn words into money.

Now the money would be used to save Auntie's life. He had already created the story in his mind, and now it was time to bring it to reality.

58

Cason, Billy, and Ivan took a trip from the United States to the Bahamas.

Uncle still lived in the same house.

Cason went into Uncle's house after so many years. The bright old man was clearly in terror of potentially losing his wife.

Uncle couldn't believe Cason would cover all the costs.

'I will buy the hospital and have an army of doctors working on Auntie to make sure **nothing** happens to her.'

When Cason spoke with so much conviction, the others who lived in the house had more courage. The 2 girls who greeted Cason on his first day in the Bahamas had grown.

Still, they ran up to him and hugged him like the 2 little girls of a few years ago.

When Cason went to the hospital with the family, he notified the hospital members:

'I will make you all very rich if you bring that sweet woman to life. I want to see her walking, and you will all be grateful for it. I promise.'

Cason learned the role that money had on other people's thought processes.

Cason kept thinking that he lived in a story. Well, to have the luxury of fully perceiving that, he needed money. Not a little bit of money, but a lot. A gargantuan amount of money that would put others in awe when he walked into the room.

When he told each member how much money they would make if they bought life back to Auntie, he could sense a passion in them. The nurses and doctors began walking with an extra pep in their step.

It's like a gargantuan amount of money had the ability to take control of someone else's mind and nervous system.

Just controlling someone's mind was not enough. Raw intellect was not enough to inspire someone.

To get someone to do something...anything...their nervous system needed to be controlled as well. They needed to feel a sudden charge of feelings that had a spirit working through them.

When Cason walked in and offered such a large amount of money to the staff, they had no option but to save Auntie's life.

And save her life...they did.

When news came out that Auntie would be okay, the whole family broke down into celebratory tears. They all sneaked in glances of Cason.

This was no longer the same lost boy who had walked into their house a couple of years back.

The Cason of old was an aimless bag floating in the wind. No direction, hope, or purpose.

The Cason of nowadays was a tree. **Unshakable**. He was more than a tree. He was a force of nature who was assured of himself and inspired courage in others.

Uncle always had a muddied reputation of businessmen. He viewed them as unethical people who sucked the life out of creative people.

But after Uncle had been introduced to Billy, he was shocked to realize how wrong he had been about business.

Business was not just about making money. Business was the vehicle to make other people's lives better so money was the award.

That TINY shift in thinking made all the difference.

Uncle had grown older.
And he had grown weaker.

But after learning that Auntie would be okay, he began to get his life back.

Cason kept his end of the bargain and gave the hospital workers a gargantuan amount of money. In his mind, it was further solidified that he was living in a story.

If he wanted it, he could have it.

Whatever he saw in his mind's eye, would become a reality.

Next up, Augusto Land.

59

The opening day of Augusto Land was a grand spectacle. There were members of countries from all over the world coming to see this revolutionary island.

No one could believe that this was actually becoming a thing.

Augusto was becoming the top 10 most valuable companies in the entire world. It was a company that would revolutionize how others did business.

This business had merged the world of entertainment with the world of products.

Streaming suddenly became a major revenue source for Augusto. The 2 brothers chugged out films that became a critical success.

Their stories had plot.
Drama.
Compelling characters and much more.

One problem?
With streaming services, it was too easy to share passwords.

This is where good ole' Ivan would come in.

When Ivan was leaving from Bahamas to the United States, he was a network engineer. He would be responsible for setting up the internet in homes and setting up *cyber security*.

As Augusto scaled, Ivan's service became valuable. So valuable that he decided to finally partner up with Billy and Cason.

- Billy handled the finances.
- Cason handled all the creative work.
- And Ivan handled all technology related work.

With these 3, the sky was the limit.

The sky was really the limit for Augusto. The same character that Cason had brought to reality began maturing.

It became an iconic character.

Mickey Mouse was more than a mouse. Mickey was a symbol in the Great Depression for having a fighter's spirit despite adversity.

With Augusto, he was more than a character.

Augusto was a symbol for what it was like to lose direction in life, face hardships, and come back stronger than ever.

A narrative that was all too similar with Cason's life.
wink wink

The grand opening of Augusto Land had a tsunami of people rushing in.

Enzo, Cason, Billy, Mom, Uncle, Auntie, Ivan, Joy and so much more were all united in one island.

There were rides.
There were movies.
There was food.

Reporters were calling it a *must see* for all all walks of life. It was being heralded as one of the wonders of the world.

Opening day was a success.

As the sun was setting, Uncle pulled Cason to the side...

Cason didn't know what Uncle was going to say. He never could predict what Uncle was going to do. Was he going to pull him to the side of the island and give him another lesson on creative writing?

No clue.

Uncle took Cason to the side of the island where the ocean could be seen. He grabbed the chairs and faced them towards the ocean. They both sat down.

'Look at that water and the sun setting Cason. You see that?'

Cason nodded his head.

'That's God's creation. Isn't it beautiful?'

Cason nodded his head.

Then Uncle picked up his chair and turned it around to face Augusto Land. He instructed Cason to do the same.

As they turned around, they looked at the buildings, the rides, the attractions and more.

'Look at all that Cason. That's **YOUR** creation. Isn't it beautiful?'

Cason got emotional.
He nodded his head.

Writing had taken him so far.

It had turned him from an aimless boy into a powerful man.

It allowed him to give freely and impact the lives of those around him.

And it allowed him to visibly see the power of his thoughts.

Cason looked at Uncle.
'Uncle, I could not have done any of this without you. Thank you so much for your guidance. I just want you to know that I'm just getting started.'

'I know you are Cason, I know.'

As they were talking, Cason could see one of the people his money had impacted.

It was Auntie, walking full of life.

Auntie walked towards Uncle and Cason.

'You 2 are always so secretive! Just sneaking away and plotting something. What are you 2 plotting now?'

Uncle grabbed Auntie's hand as she was standing beside him and said:
'It's a secret.'

Auntie looked at Cason.
'Congratulations Cason. I would love to say that I can't believe what a success you became, but I'd be lying. I knew you were going to be a success the first day I saw you and I know it more than ever now.'

'Thank you, Auntie. I was just thanking Uncle for what he did for me. But I can't even begin to tell you how grateful I am for you inviting me to dinner that day. I was starving and you fed me. I will never forget that.'

Auntie looked at Cason adoringly.
A guy who was worth so much money, but did not act pompous at all.

Had Cason been walking down the street, it would have been impossible to tell that he was a billionaire.

What made Cason special was that he appreciated the small things in life. And that's how Auntie knew he was going to be great.

'Cason. The doctors told me what you did for me when I was on life support. I just wanted to say, thank you.'

'You don't have to thank me, Auntie. It's my pleasure. I mean what good is money if you aren't using it to make the world a better place, right?'

Uncle and Auntie nodded their heads.

Then they went back to looking at the theme park that was born out of Cason's mind.

Cobra

A Story on Social Anxiety, People Skills, Leadership & Greatness

---

Life is hitting Cobra hard. His mom left him, dad committed suicide, and girlfriend cheated on him. Social awkwardness & depression plagues Cobra's life. He begins resenting people because of their unpredictability. One thing Cobra has control of is becoming wealthy. His best friend is the Science of Getting Rich book by Wallace Wattles. Every day, Cobra reads the book. Every day, the book becomes alive in him. Overtime, Cobra has a

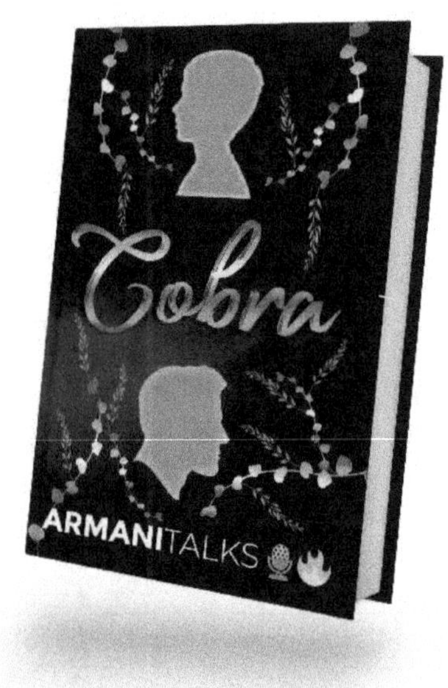

revolutionary idea to create an internet of space. He believes he can make the planets & galaxies talk. This idea is crazy. However, this crazy idea has the potential to make him the wealthiest man on the planet. If he fails, then he will bankrupt his company and end up disgraced. If he succeeds, he will be known as the genius of the century. The story of Cobra teaches about human nature, psychology, leadership skills & unlocking human potential.

Showtime

A Story on Public Speaking, Presentation Skills, Inspiration & Mastery

---

Overshadowed by his 2 brothers, Malakai looks to pursue a skillset that he can master. The skillset that he is led to is impromptu speaking. In the initial stages, he is unsure what to do with this skill. As Malakai's journey progresses, he is introduced to a mentor who gives him clarity. The mentor points him towards the coveted Golden Mics competition. The Golden Mics competition only happens once every 5 years. This is a public speaking tournament that

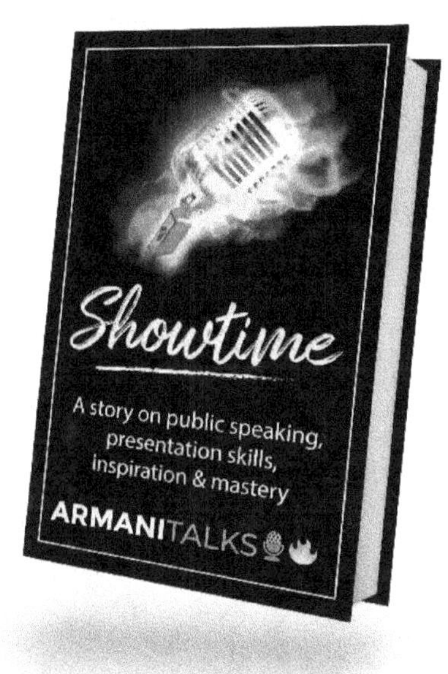

attracts the greatest public speakers from around the planet. Malakai looks to compete in this tournament so he can finally step out of mediocrity and create a name for himself. His journey consists of meeting interesting characters, running into unexpected challenges, and progressing towards public speaking mastery. The story of Showtime is a look into communication skills, stage presence, quick thinking, and persistence.

www.ingramcontent.com/pod-product-compliance
Lightning Source LLC
Chambersburg PA
CBHW071358150726
48000CB00001B/83